Skin and Bones

Georges Hyvernaud
Skin and Bones

Translated by Dominic Di Bernardi

The Marlboro Press

First English language edition

Translation © 1994 by Dominic Di Bernardi.
All rights reserved. No part of this book may be
reproduced in any form without permission in
writing from the publisher, except by a reviewer
who may quote brief passages in a review to be
printed in a magazine or newspaper.

Originally published in French in 1949
by Editions du Scorpion under the title
LA PEAU ET LES OS
Copyright © Editions Ramsay, 1985

The publication of the present volume has been made
possible in part by a grant from the National Endowment
for the Arts. The costs of translation have been met
in part by a subvention from the French Ministry of
Culture.

Library of Congress Catalog Card Number 93-79808

Clothbound edition: ISBN 1-56897-000-5
Paperbound edition: ISBN 1-56897-001-3

The Marlboro Press
Marlboro, Vermont

Contents

Passé composé

"Picolo remembers just who you are, you know," Aunt Julia says to me. Picolo's the dog. Drooling, runny-eyed, filthy, he lies quivering on a cushion. "He's a sweetheart," my aunt says while moving around the table in her thick odor of vaseline. Uncle asks me whether I lost weight. People never fail to ask me whether I lost weight, the question's in the cards. I answer: "Yes, I dropped thirty-three pounds." "That much," my uncle says. "Wasn't that way with the butcher's son, he never felt in better health than he did over there; but Bourdier, you remember that fat fellow Bourdier, the one with the job at the Welfare Office, well you just wouldn't believe how he's thinned out, he's a pitiful sight."

They all stare at me as though trying to find out where I can be hiding those missing thirty-three pounds of mine. Merlandon's here. So is Ginette and her fiancé, the veterinarian. Pierre, too. Pierre is explaining to the veterinarian that he takes little pink pills for his liver. Two every morning. He has no idea what they put inside those pills of his, but they do him a world of good, can't deny it.

Merlandon pours me a glass of burgundy. "You didn't drink stuff like this in the camp." He laughs, I laugh; that was a good one, all right. "I was saving a bottle for when you got back," Uncle explains with a wink. "Isn't that right, Julia? I'd always say: we've got to save a bottle for when he gets back." We toast. To the prisoner's health. Another toast. This is the moment when the family, bloated on turkey and burgundy, sprawls out, loosens its belt a little, gets a feeling of itself as heavy, steady, rock-ribbed, eternal.

"How happy you must be," Ginette says to me. I answer: "For sure." It's both true and not true. Back there we talked all the time about happiness. Without believing in it. We would do our pitiful utmost to evoke happiness. We would say things like: If we ever get out of here, can you imagine. Just words, so many words, so many evenings, and no other future than evenings exactly the same and words like those, miserable words without strength, which caught hold of nothing, which brought back nothing with them. To get back into the world of the living, into the whole world's world, would be a fantastic experience. There were no words for this enormous earthquake, for this Last Judgment explosion. . . .

And now here I am reinstalled in happiness. Happiness is no longer that shapeless, despairing daydream. It has assumed its precise contours, its exact dimensions. Here it is before me, massive, evident, a fullblown, meaty happiness. What more do I need? Here I am, reintroduced into my Sundays, my family bosoms, my familial digestions. Upon Picolo my aunt lowers that face of hers, as plastered with make-up as a fortune-teller's. A happiness that smells of vaseline and old dog. Am I not going to complain? This is what happiness is all about. Above my uncle you can see the photograph of my uncle as a World War I hero: his circumflex mustache and his Military Cross—for it is written that each shall bear his cross on this earth. Happiness is my uncle's photograph. It's my aunt's dyed hair. The soft gleam of the burgundy at the bottom of the glasses. And this quiet urge to throw up coming over me because of the wines and the turkey. "Looks like you're not feeling good," Merlandon frets. "It's the heat," Louise explains.

Nothing ever comes about as one believes it will. And besides, you don't know what you believe. Even with Louise, it wasn't what I had believed—that moment of unbearable perfection. Our joy—it became scattered. "Wait," Louise said, "I'm going to fix you some coffee, I mean the real stuff, you know, I still have some." The man from the gas company showed up to read the meter. A big noisy laughing kind of guy who inundated us with cordiality. In the apartment below, the radio was playing "Till the End of Time." Louise said: "Don't look at my hair, it's a mess, in fact I had a hairdresser's appointment." Then: "Whatever you do, don't forget to phone Pierre. Now, Pierre—there's somebody who's going to be glad."

The gas man, Pierre, the hairdresser, all sorts of absurd presences were getting in between us. I had expected, I don't know, probably some sort of scene from a play. In the theater they say just what should be said, they do just what should be done. Whereas in life, what you say misses the mark, you do things backward, there are always misplaced details, false notes. That is how we botched it, the homecoming scene. No, we didn't exactly botch it; but it ought to have played out differently, been something different. And it was already too late. Life was pulling itself back together, back into its old petty shape, as anxious as ever. Everything was falling back into place. I was returning to my place. I got into my civilian jacket, my old civilian pants. They seemed to fit, all right, they went right along with my every gesture. "I tell you, the trouble I had with moths," Louise said.

Because your existence was ripped up the middle, turned inside out by events, you vaguely imagine that this entitled you to something brand new, that you were going to get a fresh start. Far from it, it all gets pasted back together, fixed back up, it's just like before. You don't start out, you continue. You pick up where you left off. Back into it you go. Back into your old suit, back into your old life. Life gets flowing again through its little old drains. As though nothing had happened. You've found your place again; I've found mine as a passer-by amid passers-by, my place as a man in the street, a man on the subway. We are men, men who flow along like this, through corridors, through conduits. Glide along between walls, between fences, and everything is traced in advance, gates open and shut, all you have to do is let yourself flow on along. We are globules, corpuscles in that sort of blood that flows inside the bodies of cities. I've got back my place as a corpuscle. And sometimes it coagulates, forms into a little clot. It collects in a dining room that smells of old woman and old dog. Merlandon pours me some burgundy. Ginette flashes magazine smiles at her veterinarian. "Aunt Julia is so eager to have us come for Sunday dinner at her house," Louise has told me, "it's to celebrate your homecoming." All right. We'll go to Aunt Julia's. To every uncle's, to every aunt's, to every cousin's, I've got plenty of them. Everybody's nice to me, I can't complain. They ask me whether I've lost weight. "Prisoners of war, it wasn't the same as deportees." I reply: "Right. It wasn't the same."

My administrative director was very good too. There's someone who can do you an emotional scene. He's got one of those wonderful, meaty bartender's faces with a small hooked nose. And his voice is mellifluous, warm, deep. It quietly wraps itself around you like an expensive fabric. His jowls, his wrinkles expressed seemly commiseration. He held my hand in both of his for a long time, and he talked to me about this taxing, this cruel ordeal I had just been through. "An ordeal from which you emerge a better and a stronger man." That was exactly the tone for the occasion. Neither too much feeling nor too little. Cordiality, there was some of that, yet the right amount of detachment too. Precise, nuanced, measured inflections; a faultless performance. And along with that, it was noble. Familiar and noble at the same time. When he uttered the words "our dear prisoners," I felt, through the qualifying magic of that possessive adjective, that my five years of mud and darkness were slipping away from me. They were no longer mine. Eighteen hundred days which were melting into a fluid national resource, into an imponderable capital administered by old men with distinguished voices. Our classical tradition, our cathedrals, our fallen heroes, our wounded, our disabled, our one-armed and one-legged veterans—our dear prisoners. I tried to thank the director in elevated terms, but I got tangled up amidst my phrases.

I did not get the same flattering treatment in government offices. Of those early days of being back it is the offices that I best remember. I climbed stairs, waited in hallways with other fellows. That would ultimately bring me to a cripple from the last war, sitting behind a table. The cripple would send me off down other hallways to other cripples. You are going to come back next Monday, I'll give you a number. I would come back. Who sent you here? the cripple would roar. It's rue Saint-Jacques where you're supposed to go. It's rue de Liège. The fellows around me gripe. This has been going on for a month, they're starting to be a pain in the ass. Gripe half-heartedly, without conviction, I may add, everybody knowing that griping won't get you anywhere. We had to sign papers. We were entitled to an altogether official freedom, covered with piles of rubber stamps, numbers and fingerprints. After a couple of hours, a nurse ordered us to undress. A doctor inspected me, distaste and suspicion on his face. Hearing guys talk to him all day long about their stomach ulcers and their rotten teeth must have wound up filling him with dark thoughts. Nasty little thoughts, like bed-bugs. A black jelly of flat little thoughts, the one stuck to the other. The doctor asked me: "You're coughing? You been coughing a long time?" I answered like a good boy: yes, doctor, yes, doctor. "Ah ha," the doctor went. He looked annoyed. He brooded. He listened to the moiling of his dark little thoughts. He jotted something on a piece of paper. So you have a cough? Of course I have a cough. If I say I have a cough the reason is because I have been coughing. "We'll see about that," the doctor said.

After that it was the streets, the stores, the rusty faces of the passers-by. I would stop, I would start walking again. I looked at the neckties in a shop window, yellow, green, with stripes. I read the old placards, or else the inscriptions on the small marble plaques: died at twenty-two. Flowers in tin cans were drying at the foot of the walls. But I, I am alive, a stroke of luck. I stop, I start walking again. I walk past cafés, I buy a newspaper, there are old ladies selling shoelaces and razor blades. It's quite something to be a man alive and walking this way through the heat. Even with this unformulatable disappointment deep inside him, this stale taste of disappointment. I could be like Vignoche who on getting back went straight to the hospital and who is going to die.

7

Or like Chouvin, dumped by his wife. "You understand," she told him, "I've made changes in my life."
Guys like Chauvin, you've got a lot of them. Some
make it into the newspapers, because their sufferings
were given swift and ridiculous outlet through a
crime. And there are all those who are never talked
about, who deal with their pain in whatever way they
can, who tell their buddies about it, and get kidded
about it by their buddies. At least I will have had a
homecoming without any dramas. I'm going to climb
the stairs, and Louise will be there, wiping her hands
on her apron before opening the door. She'll shout:
"Is that you?" because she's afraid of burglars. At
night I stretch out my hands and Louise is there; between my hands I hold Louise's face, Louise's breasts.
It is true that I'm happy. But it is idiotic to dwell on
your happiness all the time, to be scrutinizing and
sniffing it in order to see whether it is intact and fully
ripe. Thinking so much leaves you not sure about
anything. On top of that I look as though I'm filing
for compensation, demanding my rights like a retired
government worker who believes they're chiseling
him on the amount of his monthly pension check.
Louise is right when she contends that I make everything complicated and that I am too demanding. The
best would be to relax a little, to more or less take
what comes.

I try, I do my best. I smile at Aunt Julia. I smile at
Merlandon. Dear old aunt, dear old Merlandon with
those white rabbit eyes of his. My aunt pushes the
strawberry tart toward me. "Ginette's specialty,

you're going to rave about it." We look at Ginette, Ginette looks at the veterinarian, the veterinarian looks at the tart and dreams about all the other tarts that are readying for him on future Sundays. I sing the tart's praises: I know my etiquette. Pierre declares that you don't find ones this good in pastry shops. Say what you like. "It's because of all the rubbish they put inside," my aunt explains. She exhorts me to have more tart. I do, I smile even harder. They all have more tart. Dear old tart.

And they come round to talking about the time of the Occupation. Uncle recounts how when the Germans pulled out, he posted himself in front of his door, yes by God he did, in order to tweak their noses. He sped them on their way with encouraging little gestures. "You oughtn't to have done that," Pierre said; "those guys didn't know how to take a joke." "What am I supposed to say," Uncle says, "that's just the way I am." "It's like me," Merlandon says. And now that Merlandon is off into reminiscing, there will be no stopping him. And as always, Merlandon's reminiscences coil themselves around Ruche. Since Ruche's death, Merlandon and Ruche have been inseparable. Before the war, they hardly knew one another at all. Ruche sold hosiery. His divorce was pending. That about summed up what could be said about him. Whenever he cornered you, you had two hours' worth of inextricable denunciations of his lawyer and of procedural costs. Apart from divorcing and selling socks you couldn't imagine anything at all ever happening to this teary-eyed creature. But it fell to him to be tortured, and not to talk. It fell to him to be shot. "You'd never have believed it," people say. You never believe that some poor bastard has it in him, just like that, out of the blue, to opt for pride and self-respect. And now Merlandon has become Ruche's chronicler, his bard. He has associated himself with this phantom. He quietly stole into Ruche's destiny, into Ruche's fight and his silence. In soul-stirring, ambiguous tales he intertwines what Ruche did with what he, Merlandon, did and might have done. It's full of implications and subtle transpositions. You lose your bearings. No way of knowing what belongs to Merlandon and what belongs to Ruche. In the end Merlandon has him crowded out altogether. Even when he declares, "Ruche was a tough nut," staring at you with his tiny red eyes, you immediately understand that it's he who's the tough nut. Made of granite, Merlandon, made of steel.

I listen to Merlandon. I am busy digesting the tart. "We had it rough," Uncle proclaims. They're heating up. They're bathing rapturously in this exalting myth that has come to color their lives. This collective adventure in which the real and the possible are indistinguishable, in which parts and roles blend into each other, and in which the weak end up benefiting from the bravery of the others. But I wasn't included in any of this. Foreign to this confused drama, knowledge about which has already ceased to be accessible, foreign to this very recent past deriving its inscrutable face from the trickeries of language and from the suggestions of reticence, of vanity, of fear, I hold my tongue, malevolent and irritated. I feel forgotten like a corpse at its burial. I don't interest anyone. Nobody interests anyone. Everyone pretends. Each one talks about himself. Each listens to others so as to be able to talk to them about himself. But at bottom nobody cares.

After each has had his fill of talking about himself the family does however remember my presence. "You folks too, in your camps, you had it rough," the Family says. Necessarily, we had it rough. Heads turn toward me, it's my turn. The Family wants to know what we used to eat, whether our guards mistreated us. "Come on, tell us," Louise asks, "tell us the one about the guy who escaped in a garbage can." "Oh yes, tell us," the Family pleads. The feeling I have is of turning back again into the little boy forced to recite Eugène Manuel's "The Beggar Lady" at dessert time. I resign myself. "Well, here goes, there was this guy who. . . "

At times like these when I am embedded deep inside the compact peacefulness of the Family, it's curious how my memories lose their bite and their authority. They are without force, they don't even appear true. No way of believing in all that when you are watching Ginette pour coffee, being careful not to spot the tablecloth. While you are watching Merlandon, the Veterinarian, Uncle. Existences as indisputable and invincible as that of things. As that of the small bronze shepherd boy on his lace doily—and having the same dignity, the same mute power. That solidity repulses and denies memories. In contact with the reality of Sundays with the family, humiliation and despair are reduced to a flickering of improbable shadows, a kind of absurd cinema. At this stage I have extricated myself from them, and from where I am now nothing squares with what's behind, there's no more fit. It's when I am alone—in a crowd, in the subway—that my memories regain their consistency. I was nice and comfortable, nice and empty, like everybody else, and all at once there's this breath against my face. I recognize the smell of leather and army woollens. Once again I feel the slimy hand on my flesh. I turn back into that naked man, his clothes at his feet, a man who is cold, ashamed of his bloated belly and scrawny legs. Or else it's the German sergeant who hoves into view. The old sergeant with his short jacket, his big ass. He stands on the curb, a club in his hand, planted there in his huge boots. And when we walk past him, he swings into the crowd. That is how my memories fall upon me, how they attack suddenly and press upon me with all their atrocious weight. It doesn't last. Somebody says: excuse me, I'm getting off here, then there's some jostling, and that shakes me free.

"All right, there was this guy who . . ." My little story goes over well. Altogether the suitable kind of story for a family gathering: colorful, funny—and with some swagger to it at the same time; part Courteline, part Déroulède. The Family enjoys and admires. Encouraged, I move on to Piquet's adventure (we called him "La Motte-Piquet") when he took apart the electricity meter. They have to hold their sides.

Only Pierre just sits there because he didn't quite get it, I have to tell it all over again for him; but afterward he laughs still harder than the others. Laughing so hard must be bad for his liver. And so, as I go on about them, my fifty months of captivity are transformed into a great big campfire joke, into a game of hide-and-seek played with our guards. That's what I'll have brought back from my trip: a half-dozen anecdotes that will tickle the Family at the end of some family dinners.

To come forth with my true memories is out of the question. To begin with, they are wanting in nobility. Actually they are rather on the disgusting side. They smell of urine and shit. To the Family they would appear in bad taste. They aren't things you display to other people. You keep them inside yourself, packed close together, locked up tight, pictures for you alone, like obscene photos stashed in a wallet behind the bills to pay and the identity cards. And then too people have become very difficult regarding the suffering of others. For them to understand it, and even then, suffering has to bleed and scream until it has them ready to throw up. But all the likes of us have to offer is some lousy down-at-the-heels third-rate suffering, stagnant and flabby. Not the least bit dramatic or heroic. A suffering you can't be proud of. A few kicks in the behind, a few clouts from rifle-butts, that doesn't amount to much when all is said and done. The experience of humiliation doesn't amount to much. Except for the one who sees it from the inside, of course; for him it is something he'll not

13

get over. Once a certain confidence you have had both in yourself and in mankind has been ruined, there is no remedy for it.

The sergeant who used to hit us, in Belgium, didn't have the twisted face of a torturer. He was a placid man who felt we weren't walking fast enough. So he would hit us. And he could well have been thinking about other things, about a garden, about an evening dating from his boyhood. Maybe he wasn't thinking about anything at all. Did he even see us? He would strike when he felt like it, swinging in whatever direction, without anger. Had he been angry that would have been different. Without relish either: it really didn't seem to be giving him any fun. He must have lacked imagination. He would hit us with great indifference, the way you whack animals to get them to move ahead. And that was the worst part of it, that cowherd's indifference of his. To be insulted and hated as men is something you can still deal with. But to cease to be of any account at all . . . Going past him, we would break into a run, despite an unspeakable fatigue. Not out of fear. No. It was well below fear, it was the crazy resignation of beasts, the awful innocence of beasts. Were I to tell this to Merlandon or Pierre they would say: "Those bastards, my God, you just can't imagine such a thing." Without understanding that a man who has just once run under a rain of blows will never again be like others or like what he was before. Louise wouldn't understand either. She asks me about my packages, my underwear. "Did you darn your own socks? My poor darling, they must have looked a sight." She laughs. She can't possibly know. I won't tell her that about the sergeant. I won't tell her about the time they made me step out of the ranks and strip by the side of the road. And about the big guy running his hands over my thighs, between my buttocks. A madman, that one. Shouting abuse at you the whole time. Once again I see that wide gap-toothed mouth that opened and closed. It's nothing, if you like. All that should be buried in silence.

False memories should cover over the true until the true ones die of it. We spin great yarns. We had a good laugh, sometimes, you know. For their telling about it some choose the becoming tone. They establish themselves in the character of the resolute prisoner, the iron-willed, stern, inflexible prisoner. That will turn their captivity into a rotogravure captivity, the way the other war, the 1914 one, has become a rotogravure war, with its cynical, grumbling and good-natured poilu. But the true memories live on underneath. They persist. The memories of impotence and of disgust. We reached bottom. We saw to the bottom of ourselves. We saw to the bottom of others. It is not easy to forget.

A couple of Sundays ago I bumped into Faucheret. When I recognized his beaming face it was too late to avoid him. Faucheret had his wife in tow and had two little blue-ribboned Faucherets marching ahead of him. It was that hour on Sunday when the streets fill with couples. Couples coming out of movie theaters or entering them. Couples who were done twiddling their thumbs at home and who are now twiddling

15

them outdoors. Couples out for a change of air. Changing it to an air of delight or of resignation, or of weariness. The Faucheret couple has a "we are not in this world merely to enjoy ourselves" air. Introductions were performed. I executed some amicable smiles and rump movements. I patted the little girls' cheeks. "My husband talks about you so often," Madame Faucheret assured me. She's a soberly dressed lady whom you would picture rather well as a lavatory attendant in a decent neighborhood. Faucheret called me "old man," and informed me about his health. He announced that he had just been appointed to Janson de Sailly. I congratulated him. And as we had nothing further to say to each other, we again executed some smiles and rump movements, dear Monsieur, dear Madame, and we lost ourselves amidst the couples.

I observed Faucheret one day when he was stealing a piece of bread. He hesitated for quite some time. The bread lay nearby, on Pochon's bed. Faucheret was considering it out of the corner of his eye, and he was whistling to himself the while scratching his armpits. I pretended to be absorbed in mending an old sweater. Our barracks mates weren't paying attention. Faucheret was whistling, standing there, and I could tell that in his body, in his fingers, the act was fully prepared. He scratches himself. He looks like a scared bird. The bread is on display, an oily gray hunk, enormous upon the brown blanket. It takes up your whole field of vision. It assumes an intense, insolent existence. All by itself it reduces the barracks and its commotions to nothing. I resume my mending, I keep an eye out, I find this interesting. Faucheret advances a little further, looks at me, whistles, scratches. I think: will he dare? The way I would think about a man on the edge of a roof: is he going to fall? With the wish deep down that it will happen. He looks at me one more time. I proceed steadily with my needle and yarn. You going to do it, yes or no? Is the act going to emerge from him, break through that shell of fear? I believe I'd hold it against him if he decided not to. Come on, do it, for Christ's sake. . . . I noted the clumsy haste of his red hand as it seized the bread. He hid it under his greatcoat. He walked off. In too much of a hurry, I said to myself; he hasn't got the hang of it yet. An hour later Pochon looked for his piece of bread and started hollering. He swore he'd bash the head in of the guy who had done this. The others had themselves a quiet chuckle. Things like this happen every day. To leave bread lying around just isn't done. Faucheret had on his usual expression, that look of his of a perplexed bird. He had noticed that I was watching him, and he flashed me a furtive, fearful smile that meant: "Yes, I know you saw me, now you know I'm a bastard. So then? It's true, but what else? I'm a bastard. Like the others. We are all bastards. All of us."

Memories like that one spoil the taste of happiness. And you have loads of memories like that one. I would be curious to know what Faucheret has done with his memories. I wonder what taste Faucheret's happiness has taken on. What protection against memories does Faucheret use as he develops this majestic existence of his between the little girls with ribbons and the lavatory attendant. Because in point of fact he is one of those men I saw to the bottom of: like those basins you empty and that disclose their green slime and all that soft filth.

I met him in June 1940. We were then hundreds of thousands of vanquished men flowing slowly along the roads of France and Belgium. An immense river of defeat. Each one was a small amount of defeat. Everything that holds together to make up a man had loosened and snapped. No more self-control. No more restraint. The swing was toward abjectness. Begging, rags, filth won acceptance. We fought to get a drink of water. People tossed us bits of bread. Twenty of us would rush for it, there would be a horrible, silent struggle. Twenty men become one convulsive beast that the sentries beat apart with their rifle butts. We filched from gardens and hedgerows. We toted absurd bundles. The Germans drove this herd along with loud yells. It gave off a terrible smell of straw, of skin and of wretched fatigue. In the evening we would be penned into fields, inside burnt out factories. Each man relieved himself wherever he could, and afterward we would sleep amid our dejecta. And the next morning we would be off again. We couldn't stand it anymore. Yet we advanced even so, swearing, moaning, our thighs rubbed raw, our feet wrecked, our stomachs in knots, our brains in tatters. And behind the windowpanes of houses, children, with dizzied eyes, watched this monstrous procession hobble past.

It was in the midst of all this that I met Faucheret. I imagine he had got some old whiff of Virgil or Livy coming from me. That was what lured him over. He was a fairly prominent figure in the academic world. A professor *agrégé,* a graduate of the Ecole Normale Supérieure, author of a monumental dissertation on I don't know which third century Latin poet. But Latin, Greek, and the *agrégation* don't suffice for everything. Faucheret was lamentable. In this world of grime and neglect he achieved a dirtiness that was astounding. A black ring around his mouth, an ignoble face, a thick smudge of dust, sweat and hair. Redheads are still less able to get by without washing than other people. Faucheret had ceased to wash himself, had stopped shaving. "Can't take any more," he'd repeat stupidly, "I've had it." Elegance of expression, he had renounced that too. He'd renounced everything. Even with a kind of dark satisfaction, as if he had at last established himself at his true level and within his true nature. He cared not at all, at this point, about the classics, ancient or modern. He had enough. He whimpered. He dragged his feet. We both dragged our feet in this nightmarish parade. No way of getting rid of him. I truly would have liked to though. Fatigue, hunger, fever, disgust, I didn't need anything further. No desire to take on somebody else's share. But Faucheret hung on to me, clung to my side. He never lost his grip on me. We must have made a curious couple. I've had it, had it, had it, Faucheret would say. I would count my steps with maniacal obstinacy. One, two, three, four, five. The heat was atrocious. I kept counting: thirteen, fourteen, fifteen. Up to a hundred. At a hundred I would start over again. I tried to figure out how many footsteps there were in a kilometer. If one footstep is makes, let's say, sixty centimeters . . . "I've had it," Faucheret kept saying, "I'm going to dive into a ditch." I'd answer: "We're almost there, you'll get a rest." One, two, three, four, five, six. Another step, another. If one step makes sixty centimeters. I would get lost in my calculations. I couldn't find my way out of them. And all the time this vacillating phantom next to me. "We're all going to croak," Faucheret kept saying. That may very well be. One, two, three, four. "Try to hold on a little longer, we're about there." Twenty-seven, twenty-eight, twenty-nine. Since the very beginning, an entire past of footsteps, one, two, three, four, five, five steps, each sixty centimeters long, since the very beginning that whining voice, I've had it, every last one of us is going to die, I'm going to throw myself in a ditch. No, you aren't going to do that, man, we're getting closer, you see. If only I could get free of this guy I'd have more strength, I'd have my strength just for myself. We'll make it through, you'll see. He reels along, his bundle on his shoulder. I'll never be free of him. Give me your stuff for a minute. We'll make it, sure we will. I'm telling you I've had it. I'm telling you they want to make us all croak. They're going to have our skins. Might as well end it right now. Then I would suddenly lose my temper: to hell with you already, croak if you want to croak, that'll mean one damned fat-head the less. Then he would keep behind me, I wouldn't see any more of him, it would be a relief. One, two, three, four, five. There were thousands of us trudging through the summer glare, across the dead plain. We stumbled into each other like drunkards, like the blind. And Faucheret would be back at my side, materializing out of who knows where, disheveled, dazed, staggering. And in his voice of a child, of a lunatic he would repeat: I've had it, you get me? I've had it. . . ."

His trousers were torn everywhere. Through the holes you could see his dirty knees, covered with pimples. When the guards would let us stop for a quarter of an hour beside the road, Faucheret would study his knees at length. Then he would take out his jack-knife and, with the point of the blade, he would pop his pimples one by one. From them some drops of pink liquid would ooze.

Faucheret went about this with a frightening seriousness, as though it were the most important thing in the world. Faucheret had been this mess, this fellow reduced to jelly. Today, in front of his eleventh grade class at Janson, he comments Corneille's tragedies in a voice that resounds. "This school for the greatness of soul, gentlemen, this 'école de grandeur d'âme,' as Voltaire has so aptly phrased it." He has clad himself again in his culture, his authority. More, he even looked almost washed, practically clean. He reprimands his two little girls who do not conduct themselves at table. "I have told you twenty times over one uses a napkin before drinking." I see him once more, standing up, noisily guzzling the soup from his tin plate. Like an animal. "You wipe your lips delicately, like this, look at me." I drink a little brandy. Ginette chatters away. Picolo drools. Life is unctuous, fluid, oily. Hair oil, hair oil. And I ran like an animal. You are here, you are you, and you are also that uncertain double upon the screen. What a long time it must have seemed to you. Right about that. You have to give some sort of answer. The time wasn't long, it was nothing, a mushy continuum upon which nothing left a mark. What fine friendships you must have made in captivity. Yes, very fine. Indeed, yes: Faucheret's friendship. "In one sense you were in a position to work, to ponder things, the rest of us never have the time," the Veterinarian says. In one sense, certainly. The Veterinarian skillfully prepares a cigar, rolling it between his palms, clipping off the end, in it making an incision. The precise gestures of a surgeon. He surely inspires confidence in the cows when he helps them calve. And what about tobacco, were you short on tobacco? "I'd say it's women they'd have been short on," interjects Merlandon, being rendered ribald by the brandy. We have started sleeping with women again. Playing with children. The professors have gone back to professing, the inspectors and subinspectors to inspecting and subinspecting. I've gone back to having Sunday dinners at Aunt Julia's. "A little more brandy," my aunt suggests with that ingratiating voice of a procuress. Well, no more than half a glass, there, that's fine. "No brandy for me," says Pierre, "on account of my liver." Those pink pills entering Pierre's liver, diluting, deadening the memories of the burgundy and the brandy. What sort of pills will deaden the memory of humiliation? "About that electricity meter you were talking about," Pierre says. But that has already been sufficiently dealt with. It is time to move on to more interesting topics. Loftier topics. The Veterinarian asks me whether I have read a book that was recommended to him. *Body and Soul* or *Soul and Body*, he can't remember which. A book on medicine by an author with a Belgian or Dutch name. "On medicine," Pierre says. "No, I haven't read it." The Veterinarian is disappointed, having hoped for an intellectual conversation. He has always been drawn to literature. He even won the prize for French in tenth grade. The theater of Corneille, gentlemen, that school for the greatness of soul. I'm telling you I've had it, I'm telling you they're going to make us all croak. "What I would have liked," the Veterinarian confides to me over his cigar, "is to have dealt with stuff like that, poets, books. But a man's got to earn his living. Right?"

Yes, a man does after all have to earn his living.

Walking in circles

The worst of all is the facilities. When I want to form a dense, faultless image of happiness, it's about facilities that I think. Facilities well enclosed within white walls, with light-colored tiles under foot, and bolts on the doors. I am sitting properly on the crown of varnished wood, in my dignity as a free man. I am sitting in the center of a dense, delicious silence. A white, shiny, rich silence. Fixed to the wall is a dispenser in glazed ceramic from which hangs a rectangle of toilet paper. Above my head is a chain provided with a pull in the same ceramic material. I am sitting. I have all the time in the world, I am at complete liberty. I can talk to myself, read verse. I can think about the immortality of the soul, if I am of a mind to. . .

Here, the facilities are a shed daubed a loathsome brown, with a door that doesn't shut and broken windows. Sixteen seats in here, eight on one side, eight on the other. And on the seats smears of dry shit. You're installed there side by side, back to back. Sixteen guys on their sixteen seats, aligned, identical, all focused alike on the workings of their bowels. Each has a piece of paper in his hand, like a young lady about to sing before a gathering. Together they strain, bleak-looking, anxious, mingling their noises and their smells. And others, standing against the tarred wall, are pissing. A little stream of frothy urine flows at their feet. And there are also those who are waiting their turn the while chatting about their families or their constipation. The brotherhood of men behind barbed wire. A brotherhood in stench and flatulence. Everyone together in a gurgling of words, urine and intestines. Now and then somebody raises himself a little and, holding down his trousers with one hand, carefully wipes himself with the other. Next. There's shoving to get to the hole. There's protesting; speed it up a bit, for Christ's sake.

I'd be happier talking about other things. About limpid things. Talking about limpid young girls, or an old lady's glance, or a poplar by the roadside. Talking about a poem, a scarf, a Matisse painting. But all that has ceased to exist. It's over. There are no more colors, foliages, or glances. Everything has been engulfed in a shapeless calamity. Everything has gone to hell. Of a destroyed universe all that is left is this shack where we relieve ourselves in a heap. Everything is empty and dead. And in the middle of this emptiness and this death all that remains is this sanctuary of communal defecation . . .

"You ask me," Ure says, "I'd say it's the bugs that

get to me the most; my kind of skin is the kind they go for."

I look at his skin: flaccid, the color of old plaster. Bugs have strange tastes. But it's true that this place is crawling with bugs. The instant you lift a plank or a piece of cardboard you can see them scurry in every direction. And at night it's all you think about. You imagine an irresistible onslaught of bedbugs, advancing down the walls, over the beds. An irresistible and silent swarming of bedbugs. A methodical and infinite reproducing of black insects. Night-time boils down to this stir of bugs. This inexhaustible outpouring of flat insects, dirty little bugs with their sweetish odor. Impelled by a unanimous and unending impulse toward Ure's gray skin, toward Vignoche's skin, toward Tronc's skin, toward Pimbard's skin, toward my skin, toward all those skins the color of brick, of tobacco, of lettuce, toward everything inside those skins, toward all the blood flowing beneath those skins, toward the useless skins of useless men, toward the skins that no longer have any use and justification save that of ensuring the triumphant enduring of the bedbug world.

Still in all, the facilities, they epitomize our condition better. Better than the bedbugs. The epitomization they provide is more complete, more meaningful. It even includes something barmy, a sordidly comic quality. To get a full sense of what has befallen us, there is nothing to match squatting butt to butt in the latrines. That's what they have turned us into. And we imagined we had a soul, or something close to it. We were

27

proud of it. It allowed us to consider ourselves superior to monkeys and heads of lettuce. We do not have a soul. We just have intestines. We fill up as best we can, and then we go empty ourselves out. That's the whole of our existence. We used to speak about our dignity. We imagined that we were individual, distinct, that each of us was himself. But now we are others. Beings without borders to them, alike, mingled in the stink of their excretions. Stuck in a fermenting marmalade of men. Stirred and churned, lost and dissolved within it. Equality and fraternity of shit. Each used to have his problems. You were proud of your problems, your anxieties. Now we're not proud of anything anymore. And there is only one problem left, which is eating, and then finding somewhere on those shit-streaked planks to plunk down our butts. Filling up, emptying out. And always together, in public, in common. In the indistinction of shit. We don't belong to ourselves. We belong to this collective, mechanical monster which reforms itself all day long around the shit pit.

When writers get around to doing books about captivity, it's the facilities they shall have to describe and meditate upon. That and nothing else. That will suffice. Just conscientiously describe the facilities and the men using them. If the writers are responsible people, they'll confine themselves to that. Because that's the essential, overarching rite, the chief ritual, the comprehensive symbol. But such as we know them to be, those writers, they will be afraid of not sounding distinguished enough. Not manly enough. Not decent enough. They will not talk about the facilities. They will talk about what their ordeal has taught them, about regeneration through suffering. Or else about spiritual energy, like that damned fool who wrote a letter to Monsieur Paul Valéry. And, parenthetically, what an odd idea that was. What help could be expected from an unfeeling, crafty and official old man so utterly a stranger to the trivialities of real suffering? The great man did respond. I saw his reply: twenty-five typewritten lines, and his handwritten signature. To tell us he was pleased to learn that spiritual energy sustained us. And indeed, such news must have pleased him no end. Reassured and comforted him. Because spiritual energy is his specialty. And when the spiritual energy is in good shape, everything is in good shape. . . . The trouble, though, is that spiritual energy is something that's put in books. It doesn't exist. Impossible to utter those two words without feeling a tremendous urge to laugh. Here, in the facilities. Amidst all these guys with their pants down, shivering from the cold. Gelatinous men, flabby, gone bad. Slugs, maggots. Hard to figure out what keeps them going. Probably that obstinate lastingness, that tenacious attachment, that hanging on to life which keeps the syphilitic, the tubercular, the cancer-ridden from throwing themselves into the river. But surely not spiritual energy.

Curious how as soon as you start writing a need to lie comes over you. It's irresistible. It is a need to give things a favorable appearance. And if you fight it, you'll be found immoral and subversive. Kids in school already know this. They're asked to describe, say, an evening spent with their family. And from the word go they present you with a white-bearded granddaddy, a sister doing embroidery under a lamp, and a pop reading the paper after a day spent at work. It's white, it's pink, it's comfy, cozy, edifying and touching. And not one will take it into his head to tell about the drunken binges, the slaps in the face, the messy kitchen, the bottle of rum on a chair, the straw mattress that sleeps six. Not one will talk about the times when he cowered in the dark, numb with cold and full of fear, sitting on a sticky tread of the staircase, listening to noises coming through the door, and the hookers bringing back their johns and on the way up asking him just what the hell he's doing there. They have caught on to the rules of the game, these little ones have. Spontaneously they have entered into the universal conspiracy against truth. Into good old-fashioned literary hypocrisy. Right away they have put their hands on the great secret of the art of writing. . . .

Fine things will be published about the spiritual energy of the captives. And not a word will be said about the facilities. Yet that's the main thing. That pit filled with shit and a mishmash of larva. The abjection of captivity and of History and of destiny—the whole thing in a nutshell. There's a book I'd like to have written. Very simply, very forthrightly. A distressing book, full of the odor of the facilities and every reader would have to smell it and recognize therein the unbearable odor of his life, the odor of his times. And the whole of his times would appear before him as one great muck of mindless, spineless creatures, moiling inside the facilities, like us, filling up and emptying out, solemnly, endlessly, pointlessly. And the meaning and meaninglessness of the times would be there, made visible, legible, incontestable. But to write that you would have to be a bigger guy than I am. It would take a guy with a ferocious, naive and generous sort of genius. And all I am is some poor chump who writes to kill time. And time is one son of a bitch of a tough customer.

To make space for my papers on a corner of the table I shoved some peelings and tin cans aside. All around me it's the usual scene. Chouvin is singing his song. The card players are playing cards. I am writing. Quiet work, rodent-like activity. I put down a word, then another. A minute, patient activity, endless, similar to that of the women you see saying their rosaries, or of old ladies knitting. I look at the card players. Fixed expressions, nimble hands. And under their fingers, those colored rectangles being spread out, slid, shuffled, exchanged. It makes for an unending dance. Fingers seize, caress, scatter the pictures, retrieve them, regroup them. I don't know how to play at that. I just know how to play at writing. I see the words forming one after the other, gradually covering the blank sheet with a swarm of insects, a tangle of wings, of legs, of antennae. Tronc says: "Pass." Tronc says: "A spade, pair of diamonds, pair of hearts." Dance of hands and dance of words. "Pair of hearts." Hearts seeking one another, hearts which brush one another, which move apart. Peignade inflates his cheeks, he expels little puffs of air. "Pff. Pff."

It's his way of thinking hard. The mystery of their perplexities. Vignoche's fingers wander lethargically through his hair. His hand is like those bloated creatures floating between rocks in a sludge of algae and water. As for myself, I'm writing. A slick of flat, black insects slowly invades the page. Tronc says: "If I play my jack or my queen, that'll bring out your ace and you drop your king." Then he laughs, and everybody laughs. The mystery of their laughter and their rituals. I write out words, word by word, word by word, words that pull other words out after them, words that come back with things from inside me which I didn't know were there, and that makes more words and still more. To kill time. The way Tronc plays cards. The way Chouvin hums. The way little Baude, over in his corner, learns his German grammar, *fahren, fuhr, gefahren.* The way others spend all day long putting together gizmos in wood or aluminum. In order to whittle away time in piddling procedures, little routines, non-existent doings. In order that our life wear away into dust. And when it's over, if it ever will be, so many months, so many hours will all amount to nothing more than an impalpable dust.

Reading, too, is a pretty good means for killing time. There are guys who read all day. Books we pass from one to the next, greasy, tattered books. Everybody's had his turn with them. They're pieced together, patched, frayed. Covered with finger smudges and pencil marks. Dismal books through which God knows what obscene dreams have traipsed. Dismal like streets, like walls. Like everything that's been rubbed, worn, soiled by everybody. Like a girl's body everybody and his brother has wallowed upon. We read whatever comes to hand. Books for apprentice mechanics and cleaning women. This particular book here, other ones there, what difference does it make? You don't pick your books any more than you do your latrine companions. You read just to read. To numb, obliterate, and lose yourself. To empty yourself of your self. To surrender to the monotonous spell of signs. To the power of signs pursuing their way, black on white, endless dwarf-sized crowds forging on across recurring plains, an interminable black drizzle, a black ticking of seconds in the emptiness of time.

Great readers, ah, they're not a pretty sight to see. That look of theirs, it's what you see on a sleepwalker or a nut. You have this urge to shake them, wake them up, forcibly yank them out of their haggard rapture . . . .

If I were capable of writing it, that tough, true book about the world of captives, to read it there'd be people like these ones here. And they'd have those faces, that blind, scrunched-up look. That old geezer Pimbard would read it. For a moment I become absorbed in contemplating Pimbard. I contemplate my reader Pimbard. He is assistant inspector at the water company. He has importance and opinions. He says that you've the age of your arteries, and keeping good records will keep you good friends. He's got a taste for smutty novels. He confided this to me with that faint, furtive chuckle of his. And he added: "But I like detective stories too." I wonder what would become of my book inside Pimbard's brain. He's got a puffy face, practically no forehead, hardly what you would call eyes—just two very small stagnant puddles. Practically no brain either: you imagine something round, puckered, buried, lost like a pip inside an apple. What in the world does become of books inside a head like that? What strange little things they must do in there.

Now Pimbard's observing me with his swampy gaze. It has him wondering, what I'm putting down on the paper I have here. Maybe he supposes it's a novel. No, you old dope, not a novel. No dead bodies, no screwings. I'm putting down Tronc, Vignoche and little Baude on my sheet of paper. And you. And the facilities where with the others you go twice a day to make your little deposit of excrements. Novels, I'd probably be as good at writing them as the next person. Everybody knows how. It's become a technique you can pick up. There are recipes for doing it, tricks—stream of consciousness and the rest. Except that doesn't interest me. What interests me is to express without cheating this shapeless calamity, this stupid calamity we are mired in. Those ungodly planks you rub your assistant inspector's behind on. At least when you're living through this calamity we've got here everything becomes clear. Everything they kept hidden from us. They led us to believe in morals, in museums, in refrigerators, in the rights of man. And the truth is the humiliating of man, man not mattering one bit. Over with, the day of resounding phrases. The truth is hunger, servitude, fear, shit. As in the worst periods. They are still with us, those worst periods. A nice sight, this Europe of theirs. Those guys screaming in the snow, their bellies ripped open, amid wrecked machinery. Those slaves being driven down roads with blows from rifle butts. And us, we who have been parked here to rot, in this village of ratty, hopeless shacks, in the heart of this Europe of snow and darkness.

We're thirty in this shack. It smells of hot grease and pipe smoke. Shouting and coughing everywhere. "Well, what do you know," Ure says, "you come from Rennes and you never been to the Tour de Nesle?" Chouvin sings songs. Thirty men packed into this place. Thirty existences intertangled like a pile of worms. "Gorgeous girls," Ure says. "Whammo, how's that? And whammo again," Peignade says. Words float in a fog of words. Chouvin sings. He's got the face of an ascetic with one of those fine-looking sociologist's beards, square-cut and blond. Chouvin, Ure, Peignade. Little Baude over in his corner reciting his German grammar. Pimbard reading novels that smell of mildew and dirty underwear. A number of lives piled up together in a sticky heap. It stirs, stretches, strains. Whammo . . . and now whammo again, *fahren, fahr, gefahren*. Pochon's having a conniption because he can't find his mess tin. Who's the asshole who swiped my mess tin? Men together. Men who eat, who digest, who belch, who grumble together. Who together go to the facilities. I'm telling you, it wasn't me, what the hell is it to me, what happened to your mess tin? Ure continues to crank out his whorehouse recollections. Chouvin sings:

> *La p'tite Amélie*
> *M'avait bien promis*
> *Trois poils de son cul pour en faire un tapis.*

And that sings itself over and over again inside me. *La p'tite Amélie. M'avait bien promis.* All those words whirling and humming around me. Entering into me. Those words like flies you aren't able to shoo away. La p'tite Amélie. La p'tite Amélie. It sticks to you. It keeps coming back. You filthy damned fly, you. You're defenseless against words. You chew on them, repeat them endlessly, mindlessly. Baude's words, Peignade's words. Chouvin's words. La p'tite Amélie. The cathouses where Ure dropped his pants. The whole business enters me and takes up all the room inside. No way of protecting yourself. We lie exposed, open to all and sundry. We could just as well have *Entrée libre* written across our foreheads, the way it is on the door of those stores where whoever happens along has the right to fondle and paw any merchandise within reach. Don't be shy. You're to feel free, that's what the sign means. And people will be found who claim that these years of captivity were a time spent in thoughtful self-scrutiny. This same time during which one is at the complete mercy of others. Condemned to others. Condemned to Vignoche and to Pochon. Invaded by others to the point where you no longer know who or what you are or whether you're still anything at all. Mankind all about you. The brushing, the continual rubbing of man against man. Of other men's butts against mine. Other men's songs in my brain. Other smell of others in my smell. It is of all that that we are captives, more than of sentries and barbed wire. Captives of captives—of others.

For a long time I was drawn to poor places. Some people, the minute they arrive in a city, they go looking for the cathedral, or the cemetery, or the brothels. A matter of taste. For my part, I would head for the poor neighborhoods. That's what attracted me. The black façades, the ragged clothing hanging out the windows, those broken-down creatures who watch you walk past. . . . I don't give a damn about Renaissance town-houses or thirteenth century churches. But I've spent hours wandering around Martinville. Martinville's a section in Rouen. One of the most desolate places I know. In order to see poverty you need to take a stroll around Martinville. Truly first-rate poverty, authentic, fulsome, rotted to the core by alcohol and syphilis. Poverty for connoisseurs. I used to go and poke and sniff around in all that. Not out of love of the picturesque: among all the varieties of romanticism, the one that seems the most indecent to me is the romanticism of squalor. Rather out of an uneasy curiosity that came to me from my childhood and from farther back than childhood. Poverty is a haunting fear and a menace for people of my stock. In our family we weren't poor. My father made good money, as they used to say. But that was thanks to precarious good luck. We weren't to rely on it. Poverty was right outside the door. Misfortune is always right outside the door, and we had to huddle and keep quiet if it was to overlook us. Ever since that time, I have always seen poverty as a very nearby reality, but unknown and incomprehensible. The poor have their secrets. And their own way of looking at you, at you who don't know. A scorn all their own. You see them from outside. Like the sick. And you'd like to understand what it's like for them who are inside. How they manage in there, inside their poverty. To understand what poverty is all about when you see it and when you live it from the inside.

But now it's happened, I'm on the inside. I am one of the poor. All I possess is some ragged underwear, a spoon, a knife. And this quarter of a liter aluminum mug upon which a former owner scratched two flowers and a woman's first name. It fits into a soldier's haversack. I wear the raiments of the poor. My doings are those of the poor. I collect bits of string and old cans because anything may come in handy. Each day I take my place in a long line of men waiting for their pittance. Everybody has his turn. When my turn comes I hold out my mess tin. Into it is ladled a certain amount of kohlrabi, barley, or cabbage. Now it's the turn of somebody else. I go over and sit on my bed. Humbly, like one of the poor, I eat my poor man's soup. And my bed consists of three planks with a thin tick and a dirty blanket. And at night it's full of bedbugs.

You get used to these things. Poverty isn't privation. Poverty is never being alone. I realize that now that I'm on the other side. A poor man does not have the right to solitude. He's born in a ward where mid-wives are trained, with the others. He dies with the others, in a hospital. Between the crèche and the old people's home there are day-nurseries and refuges, slums and barracks. From beginning to end he has to live his life in common. You play in the public sand of squares and on the sidewalks that belong to everyone. You sleep ten to a room. You struggle through a crowd of poor men on stairways and in hallways. And poverty is jam-packed with walls, stairs and hall-ways. The doors don't close properly. The walls don't separate. Anybody at all can go into anyone else's place in order to borrow six bits, or to bring back a pot, or just to sit down, put his hands on his knees, and relate his woes. And you don't even know where it begins and ends, the zone that is said to be proper to others.

Such is our own condition henceforth. We smack into others as against the walls of a dungeon. Into filthy goddamned others. Hanging right in there with their songs and their German grammars. Vignoche, Faucheret, Pimbard. Whammo, how's that? And whammo again. You're left with nothing of your own. *Fahren, fuhr, gefahren.* You'd like to do some think-ing, dreaming. But others come along and shoot your dreams to hell. With their words, their songs, their tantrums. Nothing to be done about it. Dreaming's over with. No choice but to go with the flow, do as others do, do it with them. Fill up, empty out. Talk, listen. Listen to Pimbard who is saying: concerning tastes and colors there can be no discussion. Listen to Beuret who is saying: you've got to give a meaning to life. That guy Beuret is full of things he's read. Full of big names. A guy who has a long, tumid nose, and glasses. He quotes Nietzsche, Pascal, Kant, Gide. It sounds like a string of subway stops. Pochon is raising the bloody roof. He's starting to gripe our asses with that mess tin of his. Pascal, Gide, la p'tite Amélie. Once Beuret gets going, you're in there for a certain amount of time. The meaning of life. Tastes and colors. Nietzsche, Pascal. A monotonous trip underground. An absurd racket punctuated by glitters of light. It leads nowhere and it's always the same. *Fahren, fuhr, gefahren*. He fills the whole room, Beuret does, with his vehement monologue. He multiplies himself. The room is swarming with Beurets. All identical, with long noses and glasses. And the other one with his tastes and colors. Damned right, there's no point discussing them. Tastes, distastes. You like something or you don't. You live drop by drop. You keep going step by step. That's what you're there for, to keep going, not to discuss colors, tastes, catastrophes, collapse, everything has the same taste or no taste at all, the same color, you've just got to let it all follow its course without discussion. . . .

Beuret has a noble soul. He believes in the meaning of life and in things like that. He's a schoolmaster in the Jura. His wife ditched him for a traveling salesman. The meaning of his life is to be a teacher and a cuckold. With those glasses and that drippy nose of

his, he reminds me of Salavin, the character in Duhamel's novels. Another noble soul, Duhamel. How
affecting it would be, captivity viewed as seen by him.
One uniform block of friendship and tenderness. In it
everybody would be drunk on goodwill, swimming in
the warm milk of human kindness. There once was a
time I was taken in by that inane rhetoric. But I'm
cured. I can't stand noble souls anymore. I can't stand
other people anymore. Neither Beuret, nor Pochon,
nor Vignoche. Especially Vignoche, who's always going on to me about this notary uncle of his. What the
hell does he expect it to matter to me that his uncle's
a notary? Vignoche acts like a patroness. He's constantly snuffling. Humph, humph. It's repulsive. I
can't stand him. Nobody can stand anybody. Sometimes we look like we're getting along. We chuckle at
the same obscenities. We pass each other snapshots of
kids. We play cards. But lurking beneath the surface is
hatred, a patient, painstaking, subtle, meticulous hatred. The bitter spitefulness of a bureaucrat or old
lady. Day after day we sharpen, we recook, we perfect
our grievances and our repulsions. It couldn't be otherwise. It's because of this being churned up all of us
together in this stinking shithouse poverty, starving to
death, bored to death. Others get to us just by always
being there. They get to us by having the faces they
have, the voices they have, the tastes and distastes
they have, by taking up the space they take up, by
saying what they say, by singing what they sing, by
Nietzsche, by la p'tite Amélie, by snuffling, by belch-
ing, by existing. We blame them for all that, upon

them we blame this unchanging, inescapable existence in which our own existence comes to pieces. And
at every moment of the day or night antipathies erupt
into preposterous disputes. We don't even know why.
Over a stool, a mess tin, a pinch of tobacco or a slice
of sausage. With the sausage it never fails. We get it
once or twice a week. It's a shiny, reddish object, a
sort of enormous phallus. Inside it's gritty and shit-
colored. When the sausage is handed out, there's always somebody who thinks he didn't get his share
and who starts griping. Come on for Christ's sake,
just take a look at this. The next minute everybody
else is in the picture. Ure, Peignade, Tronc, the cuckold, the patroness. All right, let's see yours, come on,
let's see it! You want to compare? Maybe I'm the one
who gobbled up your sausage, there're some pretty
slick bastards around here, me, I'd say it's always the
same ones who get screwed, shut your trap, you're
saying that so as I can hear it, and so if you don't like
it, and besides what damned business is it of yours,
you know where you can stick it, man, I'm telling
you . . .

These people were Good People. Solid middle-class
people, with incomes, decorations, diplomas. Inspectors and deputy-inspectors, directors and assistant directors. Substantial people, with paunches, with
principles. Well-mannered, well-spoken. That noble
self-assurance of comfortable people, comfortable in
their clothes, in their skin, in their lives. Ure held
what's called a high-up position in the food industry.
Peignade is something or other at the Audit Office.

Faucheret is *agrégé* at the university. Tronc is a magistrate. These days Tronc scavenges cigarette butts
lying on the floor of the hut. He has the eye of an
eagle for spotting them, and pounces on them with
the speed of a cat. Peignade, Faucheret and the others
forage in the kitchen leftovers. With some careful
scratching you may well come up with some peelings
of stuff that's fit to eat which you afterward cook in
an old can, with water and some of that grease that
smells of rubber. When you're poor you can't be
picky. Pride, dignity are the luxuries of people who
are well off. We're poor folk, and less than poor folk.
Some sort of bums. Guys like those unemployed fellows who skulk outside shops in cities, who don't
care about anything anymore, resigned, abject—those
men gone pretty much to pieces, totally washed up,
who wander off with their hands in their pockets, in
one direction or in another; they suck on their cigarette ends and don't ask for anything more. Like them
we are men reft of pride. Having attained a certain
degree of destitution, you give up trying to find your
bearings amidst good and evil. *Forbidden, allowed*,
these no longer mean anything. Words from another
language and from another world. In the light of poverty everything takes on a different look. You see
things differently. When Tronc was a magistrate, he
must have constantly told himself that he was a magistrate. This gave him a fine no-nonsense magistrate's
face, the fine dignified gestures, the fine moral stan-
dards of a magistrate. Even on the toilet he must have
shit as a magistrate would, slowly, ceremoniously.

But now he's nothing more than a sack of shit like everybody else who goes to let loose alongside everybody else. So he can perfectly well collect butts and dig through garbage cans. He doesn't care. It's not important. Nothing matters anymore to a man who doesn't matter.

All you have to do is let yourself go. It's not so unpleasant. It procures a confused impression of relief, of deliverance. Something inside us has ceased to make itself felt, a position has been retreated from, a hardness has melted; and now, now we are free of all that maintained and constrained us. Now that we've touched what makes for the bottom of ourselves, existence has taken on a remarkable fluidity. No point denying yourself. You find a kind of blissfulness in this self-destruction. All you have to do is let yourself go, surrender, resign yourself to degradation and decay.

Beuret tenderly folds his patched shirt. He wipes his glasses, and you can read on his resigned, long-nosed face all the mildness of his plush-covered beautiful soul. Faucheret, who has begun taking off his clothes, scratches his thighs. Chouvin sings:

> *Les poils sont tombés,*
> *L'tapis est foutu,*
> *La p'tite Amélie n'a plus de poil au cul.*

Pochon shouts: "Shut the door, for God's sake, it's freezing in here." I unroll my straw mattress for the night, I knead it and punch the lumps out of it. Then I unroll my blanket and I add some newspaper because they claim it keeps you warm. "Shut the door," Pochon shouts. "Shut your trap," Ure shouts. I wriggle into my bed, I huddle up, hollow out a place for myself, become still. By staying still for a while you manage to envelop yourself in a little warmth. But you've got to be on your guard; the cold is a cunning adversary. Just stir ever so little, it quietly slips down along your body, licks your shoulder, your knee, nibbles you, and after that there's no getting rid of it.

A rotten break is to be roused in the middle of the night by a need to go to the facilities. After that, there's no way you're going to get warm again, you have it until morning. Yet you'd taken your precautions. You'd emptied your bladder and your bowels, you'd pressed your gut the way you'd squeeze a lemon, to get out the last drop. All for nothing. You wake up: here we go again. There's a tickling down inside there. You tell yourself it'll pass. You pretend you're asleep; but it doesn't work. So then you start listening to the night. But that doesn't still the more and more precise fiddling going on deep in your innards. The wind is whining around the huts and whipping in the barbed wire. On the walkways resound the mechanical footsteps of sentries. Collectively my companions now form one shapeless, anonymous creature, turning in its sleep, moaning, and laboring—beset by what tasks, what battles? Men's mean little night. Grand night of plains and forests. I lie in wait for the wind getting together in the far reaches of the world, assembling its roaring medley of iron and canvas. The enormous noise advances, with waver-

ings, sinkings, revivings. Sometimes it slams like a
sudden blow upon the groaning huts. Sometimes it
fades away somewhere over villages and pine woods.
And the need is still there, and you know perfectly
well you won't be able to hold out until dawn. But
that's what's being called for. Take a good grip on it,
brace yourself, hang on. Preserve this modicum of
warmth you've amassed, inside which you're okay.
The whole camp is trembling under the onslaught of
these crazy winds. Better to die than to fling out into
that pitiless reality of winds and snow. I say that all
the while knowing I am going to yield. It hurts, it
hurts. I persist a little longer. This rumbling and grumbling life inside my body, not one little detail of it
escapes me. It's disgusting. You visualize fermentings,
the stirrings of juices, secretions, a horrible chemistry
in the depths of slimy organs, a glossy green and blue
like the plates in the Everyman's Guide to Medicine.
A sticky accumulation of glands and guts. And it's
hard at work, all that. There's pushing, there's shoving inside that visceral dead of night. I'll hold out for
five more minutes, for two, not longer. Over me, under me, around me, other bodies are spluttering and
rumbling too. Pitiful murmurs of bodies stubbornly
engaged in the hard work of living . . . In any case I've
got to make up my mind. I'm going to raise up just a
little, and I know that once I do the cold will pounce
on me. It's biding its time, it's in no hurry. It wins no
matter what move I make. I'll quickly slip into my
pants and greatcoat, and I'll make a dash through the
snow. But the cold is always faster. I'll run toward

that dirty black shed, yes, there I'll be, in the middle of a field of snow, under the moonlight, object of the world's indifference . . .

I am tired of talking about these shitholes where we squat shivering. It doesn't amuse me. I too am fond of subtle analyses and refined anguishes. I like poetry. I've filled whole notebooks with poetry. But that was in another world. Since then everything's become simpler. At home they're out of bread, there's no bread and no singing, there is over at the neighbor's, but none of that is for us. Not for us the torments of exile and the decorative sorrows. We're not entitled to them. All we have left are these laughable debates with our bodies. The life of our body invades the whole of life. That's the way it is. The whole of life, or just about. It's only barely that a few tattered old memories still remain. And in time they too will wear away altogether, and nothing will be left but the body, its itchings, its colics, its constipations, its hemorrhoids, its lice and its fleas, what gets put into it, what comes out, what attacks it, what gnaws on it, what destroys it. We won't even have any past left. Day by day our past fades a little more, it fills with holes, it reduces to thread. You've got to defend your memories like your jacket or your shirt, and even so they deteriorate and disintegrate. Yet all that seemed substantial enough, and solidly your own. We imagine we carry our memories along as if they were part of us, that they beat within us as our heart does, as our life does. It's not true. In this abstract universe of captivity where everything upon which we had left

47

our mark, everything that bore traces of us is taken away from us at one fell swoop, our past becomes something foreign to ourselves, leaves us, falls away in shreds. Some are just as happy that it be this way. That a clean sweep be made of everything, the past, regrets, hope. Better off without them. And others obstinately keep their past above water like someone rescuing a drowning man. Or at least they don't give up defending the past. Defending the image of a schoolboy in his cape, of the pattern upon a table-cloth, of a smile appearing on certain lips, of the exact weight of someone's glance. Defending the odor of a woman's hair or dress, the odor of a body asleep or while making love . . .

Sometimes one guy starts snoring. Someone else snores back. With overwrought attentiveness you follow this absurd dialogue. It seems just about over, you think you've been delivered, and then it resumes louder than ever. Protests arise. And these shouts wake up the sleepers who shout in their turn. Even the night is no protection from others. There is no refuge. If only we could count on a good sound sleep, good and heavy and thick like a peasant soup. But there are always doors banging, voices, footsteps. You stir, you twitch. You emerge from a confusion of towns, of faces. You turn over carefully. The sorenesss in your back, the chill in your bones, the cramp in your leg, they've all returned. Ill-defined phrases roll about in your head, snippets of songs, words lost, retrieved, lost again. There is something, surely, that is escaping me. Something very important. I turn over.

I feel an acidic burning in my stomach. It comes from that damned fat they give us to eat. Plus too much stuff from cans. A lack of vitamins. Although all they tell you about vitamins . . . I turn over again. My hand wanders over my body. Feels my thigh, my stomach, grazes my penis. Like her hand back when. During our nights. The warmth of her long legs along my body. The enormous weight of her head against me. No thinking about that, for God's sake. We used to hear, out in a courtyard, the metal shutters of a garage being closed. A man's idiotic laughter coming up from the floor below. No thinking about that. No thinking. No moving. Above all no moving, so as to be able to rejoin the land without memory, without questions. So as to merit the mineral peace of sleep.

Morning comes. A surly, sluggish light gropes its way through the indistinct shapes. From the darkness it slowly draws forth various species of debris. This turns into scattered underclothing, overturned stools, planks. It turns into recumbent men. It turns into the people around here.

The first thing I see, when I wake up, is my underwear and my shoes, hanging up above my bed. The shoes are without any shape. The underwear, long and blue, a flabby allusion to the human form, evokes oldtime vaudeville and tales of cuckolded husbands. Those longjohns, those wrecked shoes, those grimacing images of poverty . . .

And here's another day getting under way. Tuesday or Wednesday. Or Thursday. What can "another day getting under way" possibly mean anymore? A day like all other days, in this day by day leaking away of days, of indiscernible days, day after day, day after day . . . Time here is a useless material, an abstract continuity within which it's impossible to inscribe a figure, to sculpt an action. We're caught in some indescribable sort of slithering, melting substance, a river of mist or mud down which featureless dead men float.

The room fills with a glutinous light. In it my companions are already about their larva-like movements. Ure has set about sweeping the floor. The while he sweeps he grumbles, because the more you pick up the more there is. One, two, one, two. That's Beuret and his quarter of an hour of physical education. He believes in bedroom exercise as he does in the meaning of life. Faucheret, sitting on his tick, yawns, ouahah, then scratches himself with the gestures of a sleepwalker. One, two, one, two. Beuret bends down, straightens up, stretches out his arms, folds them in. An insect. A hideous insect with a red nose and glasses. "Shut the door," Pochon shouts. One, two, one, two. Beuret's nose goes up, down, up, down. Around the table guys diligently chew some spongy bread. One, two, one, two. Beuret's naked torso is white, humid and as though vegetal. You can see his vertebrae working under his skin, one, two, one, two. Little Baude opens his German grammar. Chouvin shakes his Russian-novel beard. He's about to break into *La p'tite Amélie*. Nothing has budged. Everything's intact. All the cargo's aboard . . . On its way toward what destination? We have been condemned to an interminable stationary crossing, to a voyage within unending duration, within the endlessness that is like the sea, always the same and always other, as sterile and bare as the sea.

This is the time of day when in Saint-Antoine-sur-l'Isle, in la Ferté-Macé, in Villedieu-les-Poëles, people peer up at the sky and say that it looks like it could easily turn wet around noon. Old ladies come out of church, carrying long black umbrellas and wearing hats decorated with jet beads along the rim. In the fastness of kitchens people pay their grave respects to the glass of red wine and the round loaf of bread. Two goateed gentlemen stroll across the square before the town hall. Reaching the sheet metal urinal, they exchange courtesies, after you, why by no means, why I must insist. The mailman, leaning on his bicycle, jokes with the tall girl who used to have a maid's job in a café in Paris. Half a dozen kids mill around the pump outside the school. At the blackboard the teacher traces the course of the Garonne with its tributaries, the Save, the Gers, and the Baïse. He's thinking about lesser cities with sweet-sounding names—about Auch, about Mirande. He's thinking about the young lady who works over at the post office and who, actually, comes from around there, and whom he ran into yesterday in the rue des Trois-Mulets. She was wearing a red dress, not red precisely, more like brick, or tango, women have words for all that, no telling where they get them from. There are hotels where you ring for your café au lait. There are women without anything on, not yet fully awake, in rooms lingering in disorder. There are the trains, there is that young girl who with a fingertip rubs away the mist on the window, and who says: "We must be getting close to Aurillac." Again she runs her hand across the window. She sees a gate, a house, a path, a bicycle rider. . . .

I know that they exist, those people. Those people who live in Aurillac or Villedieu-les-Poëles, whose mornings are laden with promise. Each morning they resume their believing that today is when it will happen, that they are going to enter upon something new and unforeseen. I do know they exist, but abstractly. Try as I may to describe them in all their details to myself, I no longer have it in me to sense their reality. They're not on the same plane, in the same register of existence as Pochon or Peignade. For me their happiness is now no more than a story read in a book. Once you have crossed over to the side where bad things are, everything else becomes insubstantial. You can speak about it without bitterness, without longing. It lies outside experience. We who are here are all aware that this day which is beginning does not open upon any future, that we cannot expect anything from it, that it'll be like the others. This changes everything. We are in the universe of hopelessness. No contact, no possible communication with the universe of hope. In the universe of hope, happiness, beauty apply to you, cleave to you with all their weight. But when you're on the other side, you no longer see anything the way you did before. It's difficult to explain. Something has occurred: there has been a back-

ing away, a detaching, a displacement, a saddening
discoloration on the part of everything. I look out at
this land of dark woods, broad plains and high winds,
this sky of ash and plaster: it doesn't touch me anymore. It's on the other side. The side of hope. It
doesn't involve me. This is probably how the world
deteriorates and empties before the eyes of the elderly.
This must be the way you enter upon the indifference
of death.

And even Pochon or Peignade, I'm not all that sure
they exist. And they themselves aren't sure of it. They
no longer have, as something to cling to, those refer-
ence points that used to confirm them in their consciousness of being themselves. The Germans have
taken away our identification papers, those cards,
covered with signatures and stamps and seals, that
were the official proof of our existence. With that
stuff in your wallet you're okay. You've got a place all
of your own. At present we wear numbers. I am number 995. Pochon is 996. Baude, 997. No reason why
I should have this number instead of another. I am
not more myself than I am somebody else. All identical, men without papers, without places, without
presence. Before, we counted a little in the world.
After us there followed a little wake of respect and
tipped hats. We had clients, customers, pupils, workers, wives, people who were our dependents, whom
we could make suffer, whom we could slap with a
two-hour detention, or with two months behind bars.
Those are the things that provide you with the cer-
tainty you exist. Tronc would verify his existence in

the blinking eyes, in the strangled or insolent voice of the accused standing between two policemen. And Ure, whenever Roro, his mistress, would cry because he was talking about dumping her, Ure would feel himself fully Ure, Monsieur Ure, a fearsome, imposing presence. Now he's number 1221. Pimbard is number 1222. He's not Deputy Inspector at the Water Department anymore. Once upon a time he participated in the powerful reality of the Water Company. You could entertain no doubts about the Water Company. You could entertain no doubts about Pimbard. He had his photograph hanging in the dining room. That also is a piece of indisputable evidence. He would look at his photo. He would see his life, dense and distinct. That's me up there, I'm Pimbard. At family meals we tell the story about my car accident, my argument with the elevator operator. I exist. Stamped into the material society is composed of was a mark which had the form of Pimbard. But they have torn us from our families, our professions, from everything that delineated and affirmed us from without. They've mixed us up together, homogenized us. They've assigned us this arbitrary designation: number 998, number 1222. A number on a sack of guts, that's all we have left of reality. And a few memories that are fading away. That still constitutes a life, if you wish, but a dubious and unanchored life, lacking in volume and resistance.

Our guards don't seem convinced of our existence either. They count us two or three times a day. An odd ceremony. We report, tousled and tattered, done up in old woollen odds and ends, with bitter expressions and on wobbly legs. We line up alongside each other. *Funf, funf*, shout the sentries, holding up the widespread fingers of one hand. We unhurriedly compose what are more or less ranks and files. Sloppy and shifting ones: those behind shove those in front, and everybody is hopping first on one foot, then on the other in order to get warm. The Lager-Offizier starts counting. He's a fat man who's lost weight. He's got a lot of excess skin, and it hangs everywhere in folds, in pouches, in wattles. He trains his big globulous eyes upon us. But he doesn't see us. You don't see numbers, you think them. He doesn't perceive us as a concrete presence, we are an addition, a multiplication he performs in his mind. Seven, eight, nine, ten, ten times five makes fifty, and fifty which makes one hundred, and thirty-seven one hundred and thirty-seven. No, no; he makes a mistake. He's got too many or not enough. He starts again. *Funf, funf*, the sentries shout. In the end the Lager-Offizier goes into a snarling rage that sets all his pouches and wattles a-tremble. But it's not the rage of a man furious at other men, it is an accountant's anger at numbers. Those dark files on the snow-covered plain, for him it's an operation of arithmetic on paper. In the operation something's been done wrong, he starts it over. The rest of us wait, our skin glazed from the cold, our shoulders hunched. "Shit," Peignade says, "we're in for three quarters of an hour of this." "The son of a bitch wants to see us die out here," Pochon says. Pochon says that, but he doesn't actually think it. If he were to die out here, that, as he perfectly well knows, would simply mean one less figure in the operation. The Lager-Offizier does not felt hatred toward us, nor contempt. We're not adversaries, beings whose plans and sufferings might matter. Just numbers. Not guys who are cold and about whom he thinks, why, that's fine if they're cold, the bastards, let them all drop dead, every last one. No, not even that, just some screwed up addition, some pain in the ass piece of arithmetic you've got to do over again ten times. And when it's done, he's simply glad it's finished. Glad that the numbers worked out right. The block leader orders us to come to attention. Mechanically we produce a vague clatter of clogs bumping together. The Lager-Offizier strides off in his fine well-waxed boots. He returns to the world of men. He is going to get drunk with the Abwehr officer.

And for our part, roll call once over with, we start walking around the camp. Huts, barbed wire, the facilities in the center. Four hundred and twenty paces: I counted. Four hundred and twenty paces and you start again. The same paces, always, along the same huts and the same barbed wire fences, the same paces that lead to nothing except to other paces which are recommenced, which overlap endlessly, along this path without an end, in this land beyond every sort of pale where we have been put to walk in circles. In this place we make up a couple of hundred walkers walking in circles. Almost all of us have assumed or reassumed the appearance of peasants. Caps, mufflers, sabots, that slump-shouldered shuffling demeanor, those pipe-stems being chewed upon from deep within beards. Without quite realizing it, we are returning to, we are recovering the look, the heaviness, the humility of our fathers, of our grandfathers, of our grandfathers' grandfathers, poverty-stricken drudges, people of the soil, bare-assed countryfolk, poor devils who also went afoot and took so many steps, who also shambled on and on in wooden shoes, who trudged so far and for so long upon their earthen paths, toiled for so long upon their paths of toil. . . . We walk in small groups, in twos and threes; or alone. This creates a feeble lapping sound of mud and voices. Thuswise are we a couple of hundred men engaged in wasting our footsteps, in wasting our words, in wasting our lives.

It's rarely if ever that I look at my companions. What would be the point? It has already been for so many days that we have been meeting on this rectangle of snow and mud. For so many days we've been like pawns being shaken up in a box. The same box and the same pawns. In bygone days I would go about the streets and my every step would bring new faces springing up before me. I was joyful. I did not even know why I was joyful. It was because of that unending multiplication of faces, and because each face was a world of possibilities and promises, a profusion of chances, of impacts, of opportunities. . . . I have no more curiosity now. In bygone days I was attentive to men. I tried to catch the remarks passers-by exchanged. Those scraps of confessions and personal confidings that scatter through crowds allowed me to

57

smuggle my way into strange destinies. But here I no longer feel the desire to listen to other people's words. I expect nothing from them. I know that they do not lead toward any shadowy or burning secret. They foreshadow nothing but monotonous, infinitely worn paths.

Words reach me sometimes, and they're always the same words: "One night, get this, I brought her back in my car. . . ."

It's Ure, part of a group walking past. Ure warming over as best he can a few memories of beds and bidets. And everybody here is familiar with those memories of his.

"Let's say two hundred thousand. In order to amortize that in one year . . ."

Words heard any number of times. Snatches of this continuous, interminable droning that circulates among captive men.

"You're alive. You're alive. . . . But you have to know what you're living for, don't you?"

That's Beuret. His long nose has a fierce glow. And a little farther along it'll be Peignade. Farther on, Faucheret talking about his hemorrhoids. Farther on, Vignoche who between snufflings, humph, humph, reminisces about his uncle the notary. Four hundred and twenty steps, then Ure once again: "If you're talking about being well-stacked, well, I can tell you that well-stacked isn't the word for what that one was . . ." Beuret again: "So what's it come down to then? So much work for nothing?" Again Peignade, Faucheret, Vignoche. Hemorrhoids, the meaning of life, families. Four hundred and twenty steps. "Old buddy, that was a pair of gorgeous legs . . ." Beds, legs, and asses. Gross receipts and the meaning of life. Hemorrhoids and middle-class careers. The sentences lock step with the sentences of the day before. The thoughts lapse back into the thoughts of a lifetime. We flounder along, following the same reduced itinerary, paddle amidst the same old worries, the same old calculations, the same old regrets, without moving ahead, without ever getting anywhere. We walk in circles.

Pretending

This is what madness must be like. It must be when you can no longer break out of a circle of words and gestures, when you have let yourself become imprisoned there. Locked into a hollow, gratuitous activity, closed upon itself, self-enclosed, prisoner of itself. You repeat your words, your gestures, and it's to no purpose, they are without any effect at all. We are not far away from that terrifying experience. A single misstep, and it's over the edge. It has already happened to more than one of us. It's what happened to Percheval, the guy from hut XV, a guy who looked perfectly all right, however, in fact quite self-assured. The consensus about him was that he was a lad with a future because behind him he had the Ecole Polytechnique. The Germans shipped him to an asylum, and as for Percheval's future, the less one thinks about it the better. In the early stages we weren't even aware that he was crazy. He kept walking back and forth in the hut. The back and forth business finally got on the nerves of the others: "Think you can stand still for one damn second?" He would look at you with surprise. Of course, there wasn't any reason why he should be walking to and fro that way. Nor any why he should stop, for that matter; but since the others asked him to, it was all right with him. Whatever people wanted, that's what he wanted. That was the form his madness took. He no longer had a will of his own. His brakes had given out. Once an activity had been initiated, he would just let it run on. He would keep washing up or shaving indefinitely. He had to be told: "Enough, old buddy, you can stop doing that now." Then he would set down his towel or razor. He wasn't contrary. It was the same with everything. Get dressed, eat, stop eating, put yourself over there. He would get dressed, eat, put himself over there. In the toilets he sat himself down and then didn't budge. He would have kept on sitting there all day long, nice and quiet, if nobody had told him to get his ass out of there. He would stand up, surprised, meek, and start to wipe himself. And once again he had to be stopped: he would keep rubbing his behind placidly, passively, until his buddies pushed him out the door. There were some who got a kick out of it: "That's one funny guy." But most were scared by it. Because what was happening to Percheval could just as easily happen to them. Percheval had gone a little farther then they, that's all. A little farther into the mechanical, the identical, and the pointless. He was a man who had understood that everything always boils down to the same thing, and that try as you like to move forward you're always standing in the same spot; that there was no reason to be here rather than somewhere else, to be doing this instead of that.

Madness, they had explained to us, could be laid at the door of heredity, of cerebral lesions; lots of reassuring notions. It bore peculiar names in books nobody reads. It was something dark, inconceivable, in which we had no direct involvement. But madness is right here beside us. We have seen Percheval and others. So now we don't know. We do not feel protected anymore. Maybe madness means reciting German conjugations all day long. Or maybe singing *La p'tite Amélie* without letup. Or being what we are and doing what we're doing. Maybe madness began to develop a long time ago, in us and in everybody. When you look at the whole thing closely, you wonder whether, before, it used to be all that different. What we used to call our freedom already consisted in walking one behind the other in a circle. In chewing on the same cud of commonplaces. In executing an unvarying shuttle back and forth between insuperable certainties. Those certainties weren't even ours. They came from families, from newspapers. They were like this air we breathe, thick with all sorts of things, the smoke from all that tobacco, germs from everyone's lungs, the dust all our stones finally turn into, the smell of all our skins. Captivity began a long time ago. Our life is at present spread out in front of us like a garment one has removed and tossed on the ground. How dreary and musty it can be. Freedom, for Tronc, meant being a substitute teacher in Douai while waiting for a permanent appointment in Orléans. For Ure it meant taking off his pants and getting into bed with Roro, a salesclerk at Galeries Lafayette, and before Roro there had been Cricri, and before Cricri, Marilou. We earned money, some more, some less. Each of us had our little habits, our perennial jokes, our interchangeable friendships. From one year to the next we became a little fatter, a little balder, a little more of a non-entity. Every Sunday Pimbard went camping with a yellow-haired wife and two scrawny, sullen daughters. Peignade attended soccer games. Evenings, down at the café, he conversed with Monsieur Barbeterre from the Racing Club or the Soccer Association. "They're a tough bunch of guys," he would say. "Tough, you bet, and game," Monsieur Barbeterre would reply. Then they'd clink glasses, here's to you, and the café owner's wife, an overweight and jingling painted idol, would contemplate them from high upon the edifice of wood and nickel-plated metal where she sat established as though for all eternity between a telephone and a potted palm in whose foliage bloomed a pink ribbon.

Free or not free, real, unreal, crazy, not crazy, it all finally blurs together in this murky light of captivity. It's not healthy to pursue these ideas too far. You can't tell where it might lead. And besides, I'm too weary: my thinking dissolves right away into shapeless anxiety. And besides, I'm surrounded by all these guys, whispering, grumbling, hollering. After all, they're right: keeping on in this pulverized state in which consciousness is done away with is still the best alternative. Think as little as possible, live as little as possible, further reduce this small amount of life left to us. Fill up and empty out. Walk in circles.

The most dangerous thing around here is the enormous amount of leisure that they have forced upon us. So much free time invites one to ask oneself questions, and a man who asks himself questions, captive or not, is done for. This was formulated in splendid language in the books I used to read in other times. Our frail and mortal condition is so wretched that nothing can console us when we dwell closely upon it. A tale told by an idiot, full of sound and fury, and signifying nothing. Phrases in books, that's all that amounted to. Phrases you could handle. Back in those days, it was easy enough to plug the gaps through which overly explicit ideas might have sneaked out. We had the Sunday soccer games, women, dough, the movies. The movies are one terrific narcotic. The movies—hebetude's grand bazaar, the sultry shop of ready-made, ready-to-eat dreams, democratic and standardized. You had only to take a seat, to be there, to open your eyes. To be a member of the crowd, consenting, passive, in thrall to the mechanical frenzy of the images, prey to the apparitions, with no past, with no future. At present we are without these conveniences. But we get by all the same. Little Baude, beside me, all puckers and wrinkles, repeats a hundred thousand times over: *fahren, fuhr, gefahren*. It preserves him from saying to himself that for twenty-five years he added up columns of figures for a broadcloth manufacturer. How many additions are there in twenty-five years of adding? And the world was full of little Baudes in their little glass cages, busy doing sums. Were he to add up all those additions and all those adders, and were he to discover that the total is zero, little Baude would see ideas form themselves in him like the ideas that appear in books, ideas that make your head spin. He studies irregular verbs. It's wiser. It's his technique for evading questions. When a question poses itself, another at once comes along right behind it. And from one question to the next, they just keep on coming, until there's nothing left of the fabric but a pile of thread. Baude knows this. Chouvin knows this, he sings *La p'tite Amélie*. We've all got our little ploys, our tried and true human ruses by which we keep out of the clutches of questions.

The great ruse, when all is said and done, is pretending. People who have been removed from life have no resource other than to simulate life. To mimic the movements of the living. We all of us set to gathering, to reassembling the debris of our old habits, of our sayings, of our vices, to putting everything back in place, to making all that into something which approximately stands up and which resembles what we had lost.

At this point I'd like to tell about Christmas or Easter, our big holidays—big hollow days. We talk about them three weeks in advance. "For Easter," Ure says, "we'll have to make a cake." "I received a pâté in my package," Vignoche says, "it'll be for Easter." The pâté, sitting on a mess tin, turns from pink to black, and becomes as fuzzy as an old man's face. Hour by hour we watch over its death-struggle. So long as it holds out until Easter. "For Easter," Pochon says, "we ought to make a cassoulet, I mean a real one, with baked beans and back-fat." Back-fat? Where're you going to get a hold of that?" asks Ure. "You figure on shitting it?" "Let me tell you right now," Faucheret announces, "baked beans, that's something I don't digest." Beuret suggests potatoes; I, noodles. Pochon keeps still. He's sore. He shuts up his bull-dog face like a fist. As a matter of fact, it's not long before everybody's sore. We talk about dropping the whole thing. "Oh look here now, look here," pleads Beuret, sorrowful on account of our sense of community, our brotherhood in hardship, and all the rest of the jerk's goodwill crap. The discussion is resumed. Ure starts acting self-important. He demands chocolate for his cake. "Pochon, you have some sometimes, don't you? Chocolate, I mean?" "Chocolate?" Pochon shouts, "shit, I've already provided the flour and the sugar." "And I," Faucheret says, "I provided the margarine." It's true that Ure is a pain in the ass. He sticks everything under the sun into that cake of his. Biscuits, prunes, condensed milk, jam. And now he's wringing his hands: a cake without chocolate is completely tasteless. Next, he complains that nobody's helping him. "I'm taking care of the potatoes," Beuret whines, "I can't be everywhere." His long, conciliatory nose twitches unhappily. Vignoche slips away: it's time for mass. Vignoche is always at mass when there's cooking to be done. Faucheret is nowhere to be found,

naturally. Neither is Pochon. I stupidly allow myself
to be roped in. I'll tend the fire. This consists in breaking wood into very small pieces and putting it into a
stove that Beuret rigged up from empty cans. This
stove mainly produces smoke. I remain squatting in
the smoke for two hours, cursing, cramps in my legs,
my fingers scraped and my eyes streaming. Every five
minutes the fire goes out and Ure bawls at me. But
once the job is done, Ure glows with pride. All six of
us gaze admiringly at his cake. It's a yellowish edifice,
very wobbly. Faucheret compares it to a mature lady's
tits. He never fails to come up with this joke, and it
always gets a laugh. Vignoche's pâté has been cleaned,
scraped, grated, depilated; it has an almost decent
look. A paper tablecloth has been spread on the table.
Vignoche snuffles. Beuret gets emotional. Never has
the meaning of life seemed more manifest to him.
Phrases from his books tickle his brain like an urge to
sneeze. Only Pochon has that usual disagreeable expression of his: he's not going to forget what happened to his beans. Pochon reminds me of my
grandfather who, at family meals, would always turn
into a huge cloud of silence and reprobation in order
to poison other people's joyful mood. And as a re-
constitution of family meals there's nothing you can
say against this one, it's a triumph. First of all we fill
up religiously, with a loud clattering of forks. Then
we all talk at the same time. We say what France
needs is a strong government, and that for what's
been happening it's the workers who are to blame,
with their social programs and paid vacations. "Paid

vacations, by Jesus I'd give them all they damn well want," Vignoche says firmly. Next, we move on to the racy stories. We'll hear the one about the old general, the one about the leopard, the one about the straw hat. We'll hear them all. Now it's time for Beuret to cut the cake. Beuret's beaming, he is. He contemplates our happiness. How truly beautiful to see men who are so fond of each other. Ure is about to break into his Maurice Chevalier imitations:

> *Une choupetta*
> *Happen to know what that happens to be?*

We'll all accompany, bobbing our heads up and down, wriggling our shoulders. We offer each other cigarettes. We exchange courtesies. Absolutely like back in the days of families, when we used to eat our Sunday chicken under the hideous dining room chandeliers, surrounded by a backdrop of flowery wallpaper. And, God knows, they weren't all that terribly sincere, that authentic, those families of ours. Now we parody those counterfeit feelings and that fake happiness. We parody a parody.

Fabled past of provincial dining rooms and cafés. That's where History went to get hold of them, these people here, Ure and Pimbard, Tronc and the others. Altogether ordinary people. History needed such people as these. It's with ordinary people, with inspectors and deputy inspectors, that History composes its adventures. They didn't ask for so much. They felt perfectly comfortable within their cramped destinies. It seems that periods have existed in which nothing happened. History was something designed for others. You could be a bystander, let things flow past. But today something is happening to everybody. Everybody's involved in it. Such are our times, a nasty epoch, a belle époque, however you want to take it. An epoch in which there are no more refuges. The people here believed that they were safeguarded from everything. They were buried under layers of fat salaries, in the depths of the better neighborhoods. Heavy doors with brass plaques used to close nobly upon their invulnerable bowers of bliss. They were insured against theft, fire, children, car accidents. But they weren't insured against History. History ousted them from their happy homes, chucked them into the darkness outside, into hunger and shit. That's the share we've had of History. We have lived some History. Like those who took part in the Crusades, or who took part in the Revolution. You don't really give much thought to those guys. The truth, though, is that they were poor buggers too, who dragged their feet, who were fed up, who dreamed of a haystack to crawl into, to stretch out, to sprawl—and to go to sleep in, by God, yes, sleep. And they had fevers. And they'd say that they were going to lie down right there, on the road, and that they didn't care what the hell happened.

What could the Crusades have been for them? What was it all about, the Revolution? For them, not for historians. For that's the only part I find interesting: History's reverberations within man. But historians, you see, are not interested in it. The History of historians is like a clothing store. Everything there is sorted, arranged, labeled. The political, military, economic and legal particulars; the causes, the consequences, the consequences of the consequences; and the connections, the relationships, the driving forces. All neatly laid out before the mind, clear, necessary, perfectly intelligible. What isn't at all clear, what's difficult and obscure, is the human being in History; or History in the human being, if you prefer; the human being taken possession of by History. Man complicates everything. As soon as the actor, the participant, the person who was there, starts to put in his two cents, you no longer know where you are, there's no getting things straight. The actor disturbs fine historical perspectives with his way of placing details, and never where they ought to go. For him it's always what's unimportant that matters most. Questions of food, chores, mail, and latrines. You're obliged to look at what events become in the mind of the man who was there. And not just in his mind, but in his legs, in his loins, in his guts, in his whole body, which bleeds, sweats, smells of wine, garlic and worse yet. The History of historians has no odor.

This shapeless adventure we're sunk down into, the historians will talk about it. There will be tidy, crisp little sentences in books: "The Germans, in the course of their French campaign, captured two million prisoners." There will be maps, with arrows and dots, to explain how it all came about. Books are able to explain everything. Sometimes it's by means of oil or coal, unemployment, the dollar. By means of statistics, curves, graphs. Sometimes it's by means of doctrines and mystical beliefs. And it really sounds as if it were explaining something; but you can't make out just what. In the past I believed in those explanations of theirs. I had a position on the sidelines; but once you're involved, explanations are regularly outdistanced by experience. By experience I mean Vignoche or Peignade, the shack we live in, the overflowing privvies. That's solid, real stuff, all that. It's weighty, essential, eternal. Outside the range of explanations. When you live it, when you breathe it, when you fall apart inside it, you can't believe in words anymore, or in statistics, or in explanations. Explanations have no hold on that. On this dark and impenetrable world of experience. Explanations are true only in the world of explanations—in the world of historians. Not in the world of History. The guy on the bus said things that needed saying on that score. I want to talk about that guy. He was plastered, but even so he was a guy who was saying things that need to be said.

September 1939. During those days everything was moving away from you, slipping outside your reach in some merciless, incomprehensible manner. Large numbers of men set forth upon all the roads of Europe, with long resigned strides, with chunks of bread and red wine in their packs, with their helmets and masks, with a snapshot of the kids in their big imitation leather wallets—from now on the only thing that linked them to their affections and their jobs, to peace. I was like everybody else. I was rejoining my unit. On the red mobilization order were the words: "Imme-

diately and without delay." I was wearing an old out-
fit, new shoes, I had a suitcase. I waited for the bus to
Poitiers in a small café where customers were com-
menting on the newspapers while drinking beer. The
men said that it really couldn't have led to anything
but this, and besides there were still ways things could
be straightened out. In there it was warm, calm, old-
fashioned. Beribboned billiard cues were painted on
the mirrors. Three boxed laurel trees marked the bor-
der of the terrace outside. Beyond you could see the
town square, very white in the sunshine, across which
an old lady in black was walking. And on the other
side, near a red and green gas pump, stood the big car
mechanic in his shirt sleeves, awaiting events.

The war was starting with this vast tranquility. And
in this Poitou small town there was so much stillness
and woolgathering dreaminess that it seemed inconceivable that it too could be offered up to war. With
despairing tenderness I gazed at this little bit of the
universe frozen in the ageless light of summers. The
square, the café, the owner's blue apron, the damp
rings on the marble tabletops, the astonishment of
that little girl who had just splashed herself while
fiddling with a siphon of seltzer water . . .

The bus arrived, a generally out of order rattletrap
reeking with fumes. This guy I'm telling about was
inside, next to his wife. He too was rejoining his unit.
And he was talking unsteadily about the enormous
tragedy in which he was being made to take part.
Between this tragedy amd his personal destiny he did
his best to grasp some connection. It was difficult. He

had drunk a fair amount, which didn't help matters. "Still," he declared, "I'm no dumber than the next guy. Poland, you're going to tell me. All right. Poland, the Soviets, the whole bunch, all right, I grant you all that. But in the middle of all that—me? I mean, me, what do I ask? To do my day's work and come home and have supper with the missus. So what's the problem? This same morning I said to the missus: I really got to get up there and fix that roof. Because for six months I been putting it off, and now it can't wait any longer. Even in winter it rained in the attic like in a courtyard, and we had to put buckets up there. At two o'clock, with me up there, here's my brother-in-law showing up at the door. Right away I said to myself: here we go. Poland and the rest, here we go. You can imagine how fast I got down, you know, from my roof. But all right then, what's behind this, I ask you? Here now, look, take me. I'm thirty years old. Or I mean I'm going to be, in October, on the twelfth. All right. I'm no dumber than the next guy. The missus right here can tell you herself. We've got our bit of land, we make a little here, a little there, it's a bitch but we earn our goddamned living. All right. Then here come the newspapers, posters, Soviets, and suddenly we've got our asses in a mess, God knows how it happened. Well? Something's really got to be out of whack. Now look at me, I'm thirty and what do I have that belongs to me? I'm saying: that I can call my own. My bit of land, all right. For what that's worth. And twelve hundred francs in savings at the bank. No, thirteen hundred. No, honey, it don't make no difference now that there's a war. Thirteen hundred francs that I can call my own at thirty. In a way I'm not complaining. There are others who are worse off. But still. And now I've got to rejoin my unit. And nobody's got any idea when it'll be over. And so I'm telling you, put it whatever way you want but there's still something in there that isn't right."

Thus spoke the guy on the Poitiers bus. His wife was ashamed. She said to me: "You shouldn't pay any attention, monsieur. He never gets this way, you know. But naturally, on a day like this . . ."

And the drunkard snapped back: "Be still. The lieutenant understands, don't worry."

I understood, yes. I understood that one could make no sense of it, of any of it. For quite some time we had simply been struggling in a dream. The dream had to do with war and peace. Never had History appeared farther away from those who make it, and that at a time when it was requiring from them participations of the most clearly defined sort. That's the distinctive mark of our times: to have profoundly disorganized the real, to have made us lose our confidence in things and beings, in constancy, in cohesion, in the density of things and beings.

Machines had a part in this. Radio, movies, telephone, phonograph: all the machines invented to remove us from direct contact, from hand-to-hand confrontations with men and nature. All working in concert to bring about an incredible impairing of our vision of life. In the past, a man's being there meant that he was there: the whole of him, entire, assembled. The same for an event. But these days you can no longer tell what's absence, what's presence. Like a sleepwalker you advance amid appearances, reflections, and phantoms. Both the individual adventure and the collective adventure are subject to an infinite series of transpositions, dissociations, and dispersals. Voices without bodies, bodies without density or weight, faces without dimensions, existences without dates. A life, life itself, has turned into marks on a piece of paper, grooves in wax, black and white on ten thousand screens, words falling like rain upon fifty million households. Our destiny of flesh is absorbed by our destiny to become shades. A mythology, powerful, confused and baroque, is being born upon the walls of cities, in the pages of daily newspapers, in the darkness of moving picture theaters, in the aroused crowd at political meetings. The same advertising techniques are used to launch a new brand of aperitif and to propagate the slogans of a dictator. The faces of boxers, of hookers, of heads of state obsess—pell-mell—our memories, feed an ongoing over-excitement. Everything evens out, fuses in the same thrilling unreality. You can no longer distinguish values, sizes, ranks. Stalin or Mussolini participate in the same stellar existence as Greta Garbo. A bombardment of Madrid, a strike in Shanghai take on the fabulous character of a break-in by gangsters in a film from Fox Movietone.

That is perhaps the reason why we are so at sea within events. Furthermore, whether it's for that reason or some other, what difference does it make? Am

I now too going to start inventing explanations? We don't understand anything about what's happening, and that's all. It's already something to understand that one doesn't understand, like my guy on the bus. The only way to preserve at least the pathos of History. History is blind and unfathomable. Ours is not to wonder about this or that. We walk in circles. There are the huts. There are the facilities. Nothing but that. From one corner of the globe to the other, from one end of time to the other, nothing but men walking in circles, guards and the guarded, filling up and emptying out. They don't know why they've been stuck there. They suppose they're paying for some mistake. That it's because of politics that they are there, or because of God Almighty. They don't dare confess to themselves that it's because of nothing at all. And yet it's far more beautiful this way, far more terrible. History finally appears in its absolute arbitrariness, in its inconceivable cruelty. You can defend yourself with words, with theories. But that's dishonest. Beuret is being dishonest when he talks about the meaning of life. That doesn't mean anything at all, the meaning of life. I'm not interested in being dishonest. I'm not interested in explaining. I did that my whole life. I've had enough of that. I don't want to barricade myself anymore against this agonizing evidence of absurdity. People have also built whole philosophies upon that. I know. But I have had enough of philosophies. Absurdity, that's not something you demonstrate, or argue about, or use as the subject of lectures or magazine articles. You experi-

ence it in the whole of your being. It's a living reve-
lation which, at certain intense moments, sweeps
away everything.

I knew one such moment when I was taken prisoner. We numbered about a hundred. Other guys
were still holding out at the end of a street. It occurred to the Germans to put us in front of them to
prevent our guys from shooting. This was happening
on a little square somewhere in the outskirts of Lille.
There was a memorial to those who died in 1870: a
soldier sinking nobly to the ground in order to die in
the great tradition of the Comédie Française. I see the
whole thing again. The prisoners were shouting, wav-
ing handkerchiefs. In front of them, this street running straight ahead, with trees and iron grills and a
big red brick building that could have been a town
hall. Houses were in flames. At the end of the street,
an overturned tank. Every now and then, the brief
flame of a Lewis gun. With each burst, a few men
would fall, and the others would shout louder. Don't
shoot, for Christ's sake, don't shoot. Almost all of
them drunk. They had plundered an English canteen,
had knocked back all the gin and whiskey they
could—their last action as free men. Now they were
bellowing furiously. What was happening to them
there wasn't regular. No damned way of getting this
to stop, you know. You think you've seen the end of
it and it starts back up again. Just look at that. Others
who had just been dragged out of a cellar arrived on
the scene. They were running before barkings and
laughter. *Schnell, schnell.* A fat fellow with short legs,

his little arms upraised. A penguin, you'd have said, a little panic-stricken penguin . . .

Absurd, all that. Absurd and comical. And full of such obvious, such naive symbolism—the stone soldier with his flat kepi, his moustache; and then the others, the little penguin and the rest, yelling to save their skins. Confrontation between true warfare and its decorative, bourgeois, classroom image.

There decidedly is a certain point in anguish and despair beyond which you feel nothing but the irremediable absurdity of everything. You detach yourself. You no longer adhere to the tragedy. There's no more tragedy at all, nothing more that's surprising or horrible. Men die, it's simple, it's in the order of things. Houses are burning: it's in the order of things also, and just as banal as the fires they light at the far end of gardens come autumn. I'd reached that point. I found the whole scene simply idiotic. We were being shot at, from in front, from behind. The group bellowed, undulated, oscillated from one fear to the other. I let myself drift with this ebb and flow of cowardice. But I had moved beyond fear. It was idiotic, period. Low, facile, cheap slapstick. Idiotic, idiotic. . . .

Their beloved Péguy

Oncoming evening. The hour when the lamps are lit over school children's copy books—the oilcloth feels cold under their hands, and smooth as water. The hour when the women of Saint-Roch would hurry out in their linen smocks and mules toward the grocery store, from which they would bring home bottles of wine and pâté wrapped in paper. I would keep an ear out for the sharp ring that sounded every time the grocer's door opened or shut. . . .

Through the hut's window, I stare out at the court-yard, at the other huts, at the latrines, at patches of white, of black, at that geometric, inhuman nowhere. We mark time around the smoke-enveloped stove. Baude has shut his German grammar. Little Baude, so wrinkled, so wizened, the well-behaved schoolboy on in his years. Chouvin bends his no-nonsense sociologist's beard over his cooking. He's stopped singing. He's producing only a subdued rhythmic growl: *yah*

yah yah yah, yah yah yah yah—yup, while using a stick to stir a mixture of cabbage, potatoes and ruta-bagas. The darkness deepens in the room. *Yah yah yah yah, yah yah yah yah—yup*. Outside, that rectangle of snow frayed by a few black bushes, by a few ragged trees. Men proceed toward the facilities, return. "You think you might close that door of yours," Pochon shouts at Peignade, "we're freezing to death."

There I stay, nose to the windowpane, as upon those evenings in my childhood. Lights flash on the guards' walkway. It reminds one of those places where cities peter out: the last street lamps, another few construction sites, some garages, and afterward, solitude, fields in the moonlight. The Saint-Roch district was like that, on the edge of the city. Behind a barn-like building that was the church began a mock countryside of derelict gardens and empty lots invaded by heaps of scrap metal. Between tumbledown walls and brambles ill-defined paths led to the quarries. I'd never walk out that far, but I knew the quarriers, huge hairy men, chests showing through unbuttoned shirts, forever drunk. Whenever they passed I liked to sniff their odor of sweat and strength. . . .

Pochon shouts: "The door, for Christ's sake." For the hundredth time Ure redoes the tally of the women he laid when he was stationed next to Maubeuge. Standing, shivering, from out of the winter and the night I patiently extract things from my childhood, and decipher them. I remember the little girl who used to be pushed in a carriage on the sidewalk outside her door. A little girl of about eight or nine who didn't know how to walk or talk. People claimed that she would remain this way all her life.

"Two Polish women," Ure says, "a pair of sisters. They ran a tavern on the square."

"You're really something," Vignoche says.

Marguerite was the little girl's name. Her parents were the Marias. In the evening the Maria family used to play a phonograph. "They haven't got a penny to their names," my aunt used to moan, "and they buy phonographs." And around my aunt the three indignant old women shook their rosaries down in the thick layers of black cloth they were wrapped in.

"The elder," Ure recounts, "was getting fucked by the army medic."

Chouvin grunts out some more *yah yah yah yah— yup*. The Pontarions also used to live on our street. "The bottom of the barrel," my aunt used to say. A gang of girls, kids and old people who fought from morning to night. Pontarion senior, the man of the house, would prowl from door to door, green around the gills, slow and shifty, awful. The neighbors would give him rats from their traps. He would eat them. He swore it was better than rabbit, and this used to get a laugh from the down at heel women.

"As for the pharmacist's wife," Ure says, "the whole battalion had marched over her."

"That's enough," Chouvin says, "come and eat something, it's ready."

"Hold on," Ure says, "I've got to take a piss."

"The door," Pochon shouts.

"You know, you're starting to give us a pain in the ass with that door of yours," Ure says.

Beuret is mending a shirt, meticulously. That shirt of his already has about ten pieces to it, and it goes on tearing near where it has been patched. It won't hold together anymore, it's falling apart everywhere. Nevertheless, there are things to be done to make it last yet a little longer. Beuret manages to sew a patch of cloth beside the others. There: that means an extra week, an extra couple of days. You mustn't be too demanding, ask for a long future. A week, a couple of days is better than nothing. When you're poor, all you are ever trying to do is gain a little bit of time. You're in a never-ending struggle against wear and tear, hunger, sickness; you don't count on a true victory, a once-and-for-all victory; you're just trying to make things last a little longer, and to renew from one day to the next this miracle of endurance. Sapped by weariness though you are, you'll hang on for a little even so. A poor man's body is like a poor man's shirt. It always finds some shred of strength for the immediate task. Afterward—well, you cross one bridge at a time. You don't even think about what will come afterward. Plans for tomorrow, that's stuff for the rich. A poor man, once he has put some food into his mouth, can say to himself that he's made a pretty good day of it. It's like the old shirt. It's like the shoes whose existence you prolong indefinitely with the use of strings, pieces of leather or cardboard. Short-term satisfactions; the future constantly blocked; a perpetual improvising merely to subsist. And, despite all that, an underlying impression of security. Because by watching your step, by not asking too much, one has always wound up prevailing over the destruction of things, over the destruction of oneself. And, in short, there's no reason why that shouldn't continue.

Beuret examines his shirt, and his long nose shines piously. Every time he darns, restitches, repairs, Beuret's face wears this ecstatic expression. The chores we find most annoying are performed by him in a state of rapture. Breaking up wood; washing irremediably soiled clothes without soap. Yes, decidedly, there is a beautiful soul. He quotes Péguy. He alludes to the mother of Péguy. A beautiful soul, she too. She rebottomed chairs, as everybody knows. She rebottomed them humbly and scrupulously, and asked nothing more of God than further chairs to rebottom. It was her honor, her religion. She rebottomed chairs with the same heart that people in the middle ages put into the building of cathedrals . . .

But the cathedral-builders, after all, were guys like our carpenters and masons. Because they have been dead for hundreds of years, people take advantage of this fact to spin tales about them. How they worked for the Good Lord, how they worked for the Holy Virgin. But the builders of the thirteenth century were ordinary guys like our carpenters and our masons, and worse off. Moving stone all day long. All day long, every day of their lives. A whole lifetime of stone and mortar. In the wind and the cold on the scaffoldings. Living their whole life like that. And the living they worked for was in order to live like that;

and the living they earned was a hard one. Their thoughts were on their next meals. Their thoughts weren't always on the Good Lord. They thought about their weariness and their toil. They thought what you are apt to think about when for fifteen hours running you move stone and mortar. They thought stone and mortar. They thought nothing at all.

I sometimes try to explain this to Beuret. But he doesn't hear me. My sentences don't penetrate his man of goodwill's woolly universe. I would tell him that one must take the side of Péguy's mother against Péguy. The side of the women who rebottom chairs. The side of the pick and shovel men and the masons. The side of those who punch metro tickets, those who unload sacks, those who put paint on walls. Of the men and women destined solely to repeat the same gestures and endure the same fatigues endlessly, who slave and exhaust themselves at it to the point where they no longer even know that there is something else in the world besides straw to twist or bricks to stack, something else besides sacks to unload, or paint to spread, or tickets to perforate, something else besides fatigue and starting all over again—until they no longer even have the wish to have done with it, with the whole of it, to chuck it, to break free, just once, just to see what happens when you have freed yourself from your automaton's movements and from your fatigues. . . .

I would try to say those things to Beuret. In vain. He's a mild soul, a spineless soul that nothing penetrates. A soul that is mildly and spinelessly resigned. I loathe virtues of that flaccid variety. My mother was resigned too. And the people around me during my childhood. And the little girls with whom I played on the sidewalks of Saint-Roch. Those little girls already knew, with a knowledge that was immediate and wordless, that they were condemned—condemned to washings and housework, to the man who drinks, to the grocer who's tired of extending credit, condemned to those halls and stairways and to those courtyards and to those walls. So many steps that they'll take between one wall and the other, day after day, hour after hour, wall after wall. And so much waiting in all those places where you wait, and there's nothing else to do except put yourself there, make yourself inconspicuous, and wait . . . They knew that, everybody knows it. Well, just about everybody. And that's just the way it is, and nobody can do anything about it. The game was lost before it began. And so it's not even worth it to try.

It's not worth it. You've been accustomed to submission for too long. For centuries on end you've obeyed so much, accumulated so much fatigue, you've so worn yourself at wretched tasks, grown so used to the narrowness, the harshness, the grayness of life, that you end up being satisfied with what you are and what you have. This order of things that would have to be changed is so heavy and so ancient that one loses heart. Nothing to do but stay in one's place. It's pretty good, you know, just having a place. A little place of one's own, with work to do, with a guarantee of some food. You know you are somewhere you wouldn't be able to get out of. And you no longer even want to. You feel all right there. You find yourself happy there. It even enables you to preserve a kind of pride.

I have experienced this. My whole childhood bathed in that tepid docility. I can yet see my mother, deep in the shadows and still, a frail timorous figure, bound tightly in her black kerchief. The frail, dark image of renunciation and of consent to whatever it may be. Work as hard as one can and for so long as daylight lasts, without rebelling and without great hope—she had nothing to teach me but that. Nor does Péguy have anything to teach but that. True, he talks all the time about socialism and revolution. Indeed; and he had no peer when it came to confusing words and things, to imposing on everybody's words a meaning they had for no one but him. There is, after all, something to be got from attending the Ecole Normale. His brand of socialism is a sweet daydream about the past. His revolution is the resurrection of the the medieval parish, with workers who would work fifteen hours a day, and would ask for no more. Ambiguities of vocabulary that have made headway since the days of *Les Cahiers de la Quinzaine*.

Péguy was shrewd. Better even than the venerable Hugo, whose cunning he so much admired, Péguy knew how to organize his legend for posterity, to prepare for his biographers an album of Péguy pictures in color. One need but choose. The schoolboy, the peasant, the reserve officer, Péguy in wooden shoes, Péguy in a mantle, Péguy on a pilgrimage. A Péguy bent, bowed, crooked, twisted, it's not adjectives he is wanting in. A Péguy like unto the old stalwarts who betake themselves to the fields, like unto the old women who keep watch over the cows. A man bred to rude toil, born to poverty, a man of the people. A man of the soil and of tradition. His great fear was that he be taken for a bourgeois, for a monsieur. That his mantle and sabots not be sufficiently noticed. It must be borne in mind that he was never able to sit in an armchair: now there's an indication for you. And that he was on familiar terms with the printers. By dint of maintaining he is of the people, he even ends up believing he is the only one who is of the people, that he's the people all by himself. "Nowadays everybody is bourgeois because everybody reads the newspaper." Everybody except him, Péguy.

Since he's particular about this, we can grant it to him. He was of the people, that's so; but only through his loyalty to the compact, unmoving and limited certainties of his childhood. Through that work-weariness and that millennial acceptance of fate out of which he makes morality and poetry. The world in which we must live from now on is a harsh one. Everything needs to be invented—the form of combat and the weapons, the myths and the gods. Péguy invites us to turn back toward a closed and warm past without problems, in which we would be well shut in, firmly held, bound to the living, bound to the earth and to the dead. An enduring temptation in the hearts of men who have long lived in unremitting difficulty, in the bittersweet anxieties of old resignations. It's like a little square after a rain, where schoolchildren play in silence. You would reach it after walking down many streets, crossing through dank, dark neighborhoods full of clamor after having patiently threaded your way through a jumble of shops and factories, through God knows what confusion of walls and dusk. And at the end of it all, there would be this little square, with two trees and a bench . . .

No surprise that a fellow like Beuret would fall for this wisdom of the defeated. Péguy's first disciples, those fabled subscribers to the *Cahiers*, must have been like Beuret, a little stoop-shouldered, a little nearsighted, overflowing with candor and goodwill. But Beuret is a moron. There are the others, those who have come later, those who make a lot of noise nowadays. The people who are in the forefront of things, serious people, neat, spruce people, rascals, little bastards, moral people, nationalist people, all those who are for Family and for Work and for the poor to stay put in their poor people's places, those who are for traditions, situations and decorations, ladies paying calls, young people pushing their way up, those who've arrived, those who will arrive, those who say it's the fault of the schoolmasters, those who say it's the fault of paid vacations. That whole lot is for Péguy. They've put Péguy on their side. They make him walk at the head of their procession. Saint Péguy, pray for us. A convenient fellow, Péguy. He provides them with all their justifications, all their guarantees. You just need to cut from the body of his work those

pages he wrote in the name of his social class and
which can be used against it. You'd be a damned fool
to deprive yourself. They've got hold of Péguy the
way they get hold of retired generals in order to stick
them on their boards of directors. They are partisans,
they too, of the work mystique. And of pride in one's
craft. And of the well-made artifact. It suits their
needs, this defused socialism. It's in perfect keeping
with their interests and their fears. They'd be on easy
street, wouldn't they, by God, if the joy of working
were all the salary workingmen asked for. Punch your
tickets, rebottom your chairs, unload your sacks,
stack your bricks, without complaining, without
grumbling, without ever laying down your tools,
without going out on strike, without saying no. In a
spirit of Christian humility. The way they used to do
back in the fifteenth century, an outstandingly *belle
époque*. And let yourself be crushed with work, driven
stupid, drained and worn ragged by work. It's Péguy
who's telling you. He was an expert, Péguy was, in
workingman's honor, in conscientious workmanship.
Péguy wasn't one of your bourgeois, one of your mon-
sieurs. He was a chap like you, he came from where
you came from, he was a man of the people, a social-
ist. So what more could you wish?

I become heated, as though it were all worth the
trouble. It's because of Beuret. All I have to do is
watch that imbecile mending his rags and I start thinking about Péguy. Beuret has rough, red hands. His
mother had hands like that, I'm sure of it. And Péguy's
mother, and my mother. The wretched hands of dish-

washing and pots and pans scouring women. He's proud as hell of those hands of his.

There he is, he takes a break from his work in order to pull out one of the cigarette butts he keeps in a can. He takes a drag: a little pleasure he permits himself. The little pleasures of deflated little lives. The little homilies: be careful, be frugal, be content with little. The mild-mannered, grovelling philosophy of my childhood. That's what they taught me there in the house in the Saint-Roch district. I have still to recover from it. They taught me the sound virtues of the little people who flounder in their invisible existence. The modest, unassuming virtues of the people. On that score I know as much as Péguy. We have some things in common, he and I. Memories of streets, of shops, and of primary school. Of ancestors who were farm-hands and charwomen. I too was once the little boy sent to the corner store with injunctions not to lose his pennies. I was once the schoolboy walking beneath chestnut trees in the warm rain the new school year began with. And in the evening I would do my arith-metic problems, I'd conscientiously learn my history lessons, Joan of Arc, Henry IV, the Seven Years War. So, this Péguy of theirs doesn't touch my heartstrings, with his childhood of toil as a child of the people. Were I the son of a banker or a colonel, who knows, I might find him touching—Péguy, the prize pupil at the town elementary school with his books under his arm. That Péguy who remained so much of the people, so faithful to the people, and so basically reassuring despite his firebrand airs. But my mother was a seamstress, and my father, a machinist. I may therefore dispense with precautions. I leave piety to simpletons and cynics. If they feel the urge they can water their souls with the work mystique and the hope of kingdom come. With all those formulae from Péguy now being plastered all over the place like billboards—"mystique," and "politics," "epochs" and "periods." (Not to mention the heads of families, the great adventurers of modern times.) It leaves me cold. In all that I see only ways of tricking out weakness and submission as courage and rebellion. I don't buy it.

Obviously, these things ought to be expressed differently. Expounded, for instance, in a solid critical study of the sort my teachers taught me to write. Something tightly organized, nicely nuanced, objective, with quotations and footnotes. Now that would be a worthy use of the leisure I enjoy as a captive. And at least I'll be in a splendid role. The role of the invulnerable intellectual, of the scholar who frees himself from reality's tumults by means of painstaking research and serene reflection. My butt on the shitting plank, but my head in the higher regions of thought. The victory of mind over circumstances. But I gave up the pursuit of such victories. Why, am I still capable of having thoughts? Hard feelings, at the very most. Disillusionments, repulsions, disgusts. You don't put together solid critical studies out of that sort of stuff. For me Péguy's not an author whose art or philosophy one analyzes: he's a man I can't stomach. A fellow who exasperates me. Like Beuret, like Vignoche, or like Pochon.

I remember a photograph of him I once saw. He's in his shop, the famous shop on the rue de la Sorbonne. Standing, with his right hand on the back of a chair. The self-assurance, self-importance of a shop owner. He reminds me of my uncle, who had a hardware store. But most of all, with that beard and pincenez of his, he makes one think of the professors of those days. The likeness is flagrant. Monsieur Lavisse, Monsieur Lanson, the university scholars he manhandled in his writings, they too had that same short beard, that peremptory pince-nez, and the little vertical wrinkle upon the brow caused by the pince-nez. Despite all his denials, Péguy is one of them. It didn't please him, it wasn't "people" enough. So loudly did he proclaim his scorn for academic, abstract, bookish thinking, that one might finally come to believe him. But though he may have left Academia, Academia didn't let go of him. It isn't just a question of pince-nez and beard. There's the style, the tone. Whenever I pick up Péguy, I feel I am back in high school. That unending monologue is the professorial drone. Péguy is in the chair. Comfortably seated, firmly established, in no hurry. He decides, he distinguishes, he classifies. He places mystique on one side, politics on the other, everything becomes clear. In the first place, in the second place, capital A, capital B. Clear-cut views, well-defined categories, inflexible affirmations. An uncompromising professor, sure of himself, utterly indifferent to the adulterations, the contagions, the incursions of reality. He glides from digression to digression. He explicates a text. The explication goes on for two hundred pages. And he's never certain he has explicated enough. Compared enough, clarified enough, emphasized enough. He aligns synonyms tirelessly. He provides detailed etymologies. He arranges words according to family. It's his way of loving the language: not as an artist, but as a professor. And there's Latin, there's Greek. And classical allusions, with a sidelong glance at the good pupils to see whether they've caught them. And those unduly labored puns. Those passages of deliberate uncouthness, those vulgarities of expression that in your authority on grammar are the mark of innocent debauchery.

A professor rather given to long-winded nonsense, that finally is how their Péguy appears to me. And a mean character to boot. Full of bitter passions, vast and puerile hatreds. Forever engaged in pedantic quarrels. Having relentlessly at his Sorbonne colleagues over programs of study and nominations. And very quick with charges of treason. Those lustreless, those inoffensive functionaries, the Langloises, the Lansons and the Lavisses, all traitors. Péguy is all alone in not betraying. You have to be someone in the University to take university figures as seriously as that. Nowhere but in the University can anyone thus confuse the Sorbonne with culture. Péguy's problems, his indignations, his denunciations have meaning and importance only within the world of professors. Once you step out of the world of professors, you're astonished that anyone could ever have become excited over such issues. And step out of it I did. Or, rather, events removed me from there, somewhat by the scruff of the neck. The experience of hunger, of humiliation and of fear gives things their exact dimensions. You see clearly that Péguy's debates with a few student monitors are of no account. They transpire outside of where the action is, outside of life. Inside that arbitrary, insubstantial universe where academic thinking conducts its ludicrous games.

Equally without moment are Péguy's bellicose speeches. He saw the war coming. He had his eye out for it as if for a bus at a street corner. Mustn't miss that one. My generation mustn't miss it—that occasion for nobility, for heroism, for History. Indeed, what he rather feared was not getting it, his "enrollment in history," as he called it. Not obtaining it, his participation in a vast, epic event. He got it, everything he could ask for, and a couple of million poor bastards along with him who didn't ask for so much. It cost him his skin. Litterateurs who had managed to save theirs praised him for his sacrifice. I don't know anything about Péguy's death. Nobody knows anything about anybody's death. He had written: "Fortunate are they who die in a just war..." Alexandrines I learned by heart once upon a time. Everybody learned them by heart. Since then, I've seen a good number of fortunate corpses. Real ones, rotting unpoetically away, sprawled at the bottom of a ditch. It's a sight that invites to unemotional discussion of these things. The dead are neither fortunate nor unfortunate: they're dead. Their watches and boots have been stolen from them, and they rot away at the bottom of a ditch. This reality of war and death contains the cure for a certain martial lyricism. But Péguy saw war as it is presented in the books which professors comment upon in class. As in Victor Hugo. As in the Iliad. As in Corneille. Around about the age of fifteen each of us came to know one of those fierce old instructors who would be thrown into a pious frenzy by the battle of the Horatii or the invocation of the soldiers of Year II. Péguy too used to be transported by Bastille Day and medal-winning heroism. Those vocal effects and those muscular effects. That rhetoric that blusters, that trumpets, that rat-a-tat-tats. That oratorical courage, unrelated to real courage, which is silence and solitude—the most silent, the most solitary awakening to consciousness; the most incommunicable experience; the most secret ordeal; a searing and total discovery of the self within the depths of an anguish that has no name. Péguy's imagery, his dreams of battles, cavalcades and crusades, all that loses its seriousness in the presence of the actual event. And present it is. The day for rhetoric is past. We too have got ourselves enrolled in History. And when you are nose to nose with the event, a change is wrought in your ways of seeing things. The event is like corpses. It is noble and glorious only in high school literature. In the living truth of life it is shoddy, it is ugly, it stinks. When you're not as dumb as Beuret, this does eventually become apparent to you. By dint of shivering in a hut from one evening to the next you do come to know at least one thing: there's no need to beckon to catastrophe.

You won't miss out on it. It won't fail you. You'll have your share of it, there's some for everybody. You'll get your share, and good measure. Your share of History and epic. Your share of night, of snow, of filth, and of shit. You're entitled to it. Entitled to the vermine. To the rutabaga soups. To the sentries. To the facilities. To those stagnant pools below, those squattings above them. Entitled to Ure's obscenity. To Vignoche's stupidity. Entitled to Beuret, to Pochon, to Chouvin. To Chouvin's ditties, *La p'tite Amélie, yah yah yah yah yah*. Péguy was preyed upon by the urge to inscribe a grand military history within eternal history. Those are his words. Grandeur! For that we'll have to come back some other time. Maybe some men hit upon better luck than we did. Maybe somewhere, God only knows where, there are characters out of Corneille or soldiers from the Year II. But not here. Here, there's only Ure and Pochon, and Faucheret, and Tronc. And Chouvin singing:

> *La p'tite Amélie*
> *Oua oua oua oua oua*
> *M'avait bien promis*
> *Yah yah yah yah—yup*

Our noble profession

The Russian camp is three hundred meters from ours.
Our pastime, that summer, was watching the Russians being buried. A very monotonous undertaking.
Hauling the cart loaded with corpses. Dragging the
corpses out. Dumping the corpses into the pit. Doing
it again. Doing that all day long. Handling dead men
all day long. Upon that expanse of sand and sunlight.
All day long trotting that ramshackle cart back and
forth between the camp and the pit. The living who
did that hadn't much more life in them than the dead
they were dealing with: just the amount required to
walk, to push a little, to pull a little. Men with un-
seeing eyes. Men with nothing to them. Men at a
remove from everything. And to guard them, the dead
and the nearly dead, two sentries who mainly whis-
tled. Two fellows who didn't give a shit. Whether
they were doing this or something else. They would
be saying to themselves that what the hell, it isn't

worse here than than at the front. Right here, in the sand and sunlight. From time to time they would let out threatening yells. They would cut loose with their rifle butts, a jab here, a jab there. With no mean intentions, but because, you know, that was the sort of job they had. And because, you know, it feels good to be alive. Anyway, Russians aren't affected by blows and insults. That's the way they are. One indeed wonders what could still have an effect upon the Russians. They move their feet forward. They perform their movements. But they are no longer on this side of things. They drift with supernatural slowness through a ghostly universe. And it is they, those ones who are alive, who evoke ideas of death. Not the dead. The dead are so dead that they already belong to the world of stone, of wood. You say to yourself that it is heavy, that it is cold, you do not say to yourself that it is a man. And then there are too many of them, too many of the dead. A corpse, you can cope with that. Standing before an unknown cadaver, your thoughts stray, you repeat old phrases to yourself. But when it is dead bodies by whole cartloads, pits filled to the brim with dead bodies, and that all day long, and for days and days, well, you run out of words and ideas for it. All you can do is look. Dead bodies stripped naked, white, their heads lolling, their dislocated arms dangling. Intertwined dead bodies, and to disentangle them, to pry them apart was quite a business. And then they'd be placed on a stretcher. On each side their arms would hang down, swaying. Dead bodies so thin you couldn't believe your eyes. Splashes of dark blood on some, those the Germans had machine-gunned. Others splattered with excrement: the ones who had died from dysentery. The living advanced with the gait of sleepwalkers. They appeared to be moving within an invisible substance, horribly thick and heavy. Four would team up in order to carry a dead body. Truly grotesque in their moss-colored overcoats with overlong sleeves. Grotesque phantoms. When they would reach the edge of the pit, they would tip the body off the stretcher, then would go off to get another. Like that indefinitely. The dead body would fall in whatever way, crookedly. In each pit three hundred dead bodies had to be lodged. Three hundred, not one less. How that was to be accomplished was strictly up to the dead and the living. A German non-commissioned officer kept count. He was a man richly provided with cheeks, chins, buttocks. A fine-looking German non-commissioned officer, polished, shaven, gleaming, and conscientious. He was holding pencil and paper. He counted his dead carefully. One hundred seventy-six, one hundred seventy-seven, one hundred seventy-eight. Without making a mistake. A perfectly regulated machine. And, for all that, a real human being, a man who perspired, who smoked a cigar. One hundred seventy-nine, one hundred eighty. For the Russians lugging them about, the dead bodies caked with dried blood were something heavy to lug about. For the non-commissioned officer, they were numbers. One hundred eighty-one, one hundred eighty-two . . . Three hundred per pit. Five, six, seven pits. Adding, multiplying, writing down the figures on his sheets of paper. Everything was by the book, clean and clear in this universe of statistics that the non-commissioned officer inhabited. A responsible man, who was fulfilling his obligations, as was proper. The dead had simply to fulfill theirs. The dead had simply to settle themselves inside their pit in quantities of three hundred. Which wasn't easy, for the size of the hole had been rather closely calculated. But the non-commissioned officer saw to it that the dead were tightly packed. He would order a Russian down into the pit to trample the dead bodies so as to get everything in that happened to be sticking out, heads, arms, and so the Russian walked on top of the heads, arms, until all that was tightly compressed, leveled, without the least bit of wasted space. Method, that's what it was all about. Thanks to his method the non-commissioned officer's figures were exact. Three hundred per pit, neither more nor less. Three hundred.

It was right at the time of the Russians. I'd picked up an old newspaper from the table. I had seen that. I had thought: "Well, what do you know . . ." Because all it amounted to was one more dead body. One gray, broken, dead body, caked over with dark blood. The same as the Russians. The same as all dead bodies. Naked, impersonal. A dead body that had been heaved that way, one, two, on top of the other dead bodies. Into a pit. Jews and communists, the paper said. Hostages who had been shot. A few corpses added to all the corpses in these days of corpses. And that one among the others, it was really him, the paper gave his last name, his first name, his date of birth: Gokelaere (Albert), born in 1915.

My pupil Gokelaere. . . . For he had been my pupil, ten years before. A skinny, timid little fellow who would get flustered and stutter whenever I asked him a question. He had a seat in the third row, by a window, from which you could see two trees and a wall. That is pretty much all I knew about him then. There were thirty or forty in his class. Sixteen-year-old boys, youthful males, small-minded, crafty, and tough. Forty brains to fill with history, algebra. According to how much more or less they were able to contain you took more or less interest in them. This could be expressed numerically, it was a convenient way: so much out of twenty. That's what teachers are there for. To correct assignments, to comment upon Pascal or Bossuet, to prepare pupils for exams. I did my job exactly. For me Gokelaere was the pupil in the third row beside the window. Gokelaere was a name in my grade book, in its alphabetic place, between the Fs and the Hs, and adjoining his name there were columns, composition, *explication de texte*, and numbers in the columns. Everything was in proper order. I like having everything in proper order. I am a functionary. I am punctilious. They are very punctilious in the university. Punctiliously you retail your dates in history, your rules of grammar, your quotations from Virgil. Like the grocer who weighs out cooking salt and grated cheese. Or else like a good quartermaster who counts shoes, rations, or corpses. From quartermasters and teachers that's all anyone has a right to ask. The teacher has his forty pupils. These particular ones or some others, it is of no importance. Forty every year, year in year out, over a period of some thirty years. Beyond that there's nothing you need bother over. You have a clear conscience. In the evenings, you go out and hold forth at the Café de la Bourse, like my colleague Dardillon. Or else you prepare a thesis on Crébillon fils, like my colleague Cercote. You're seemly and have a good record. You're a scrupulous bureaucrat, gone soft about the body, respectful of ritual. You correct translations. You tot up misconstructions, solecisms. You do your job. And everything a boy of sixteen can secrete in the way of anguish and heartbreak, well, that's not our job. Nor is to exert an influence upon those futures already budding and uncertain. That has nothing to do with the programs leading to the *baccalauréat*. And then it's too serious a business; correcting translations implies less in the way of responsibilities. Thus does one contrive to live among adolescents without even an inkling of who they are. Wrapped in your respectable bearing you sail through those haunted, wretched regions of the awkward age with the professional indifference of an undertaker or a physician in a charity ward.

And yet a rent may develop in this universe of appearances where teachers station themselves. They may be made witness to one of those startling gestures which tear a hole in the fabric. Like that time when a little eleventh grader ran away from school.

Nobody had ever suspected a thing. He was so well-behaved, so retiring, so unremarkable. Not much in mathematics, the mathematics teacher said. Not too bad in English, the English teacher said. What's called your average pupil. And look what the little fellow had gone and done. It was more than anyone could understand. One evening he left, and all night long he wandered somewhere or other about the countryside. For the whole of a night he had the whole night and the whole countryside all to himself, with their animals and their stars. And in the morning he threw himself into a pond. His books and copy-books were neatly arranged inside his desk. But he left behind nothing shedding light upon his tragedy. No thin little notebook of the kind in which childhood attempts to sort out its chances and its strengths. Not even the letter that begins with "When you read these lines, I shall be dead." He had covered over his footsteps and taken away all the keys. When those things happen, you wonder whether carefully correcting translations was enough. You see them there, those living shadows, hovering about this youthful body, to which death gives such weight. The Dardillons, the Cercotes, with their briefcases and their jackets, with their old men's faces, yellowed or blotched, loaded over with beard and pince-nez. They peer down upon these now closed waters in whose depths tremble the fatalities and the phantoms of adolescence. For once in their lives they inquire of themselves, feel uneasy, feel afraid. They visualize strange inward debates and struggles, glimpse hidden existences, strained and unhappy. You are never entirely safeguarded against tragedy. Even in a classroom it ends up having at you. Yet God knows that, teachers or not, men have little fondness for that, for tragedy. Except in the theater, of course. And that we humans find a way, that we take detours to avoid it, to notice nothing whatsoever. Otherwise we would never have any peace of mind at all. We walk amid houses, amid people; we don't ask ourselves what lies hidden behind walls and expressions. Because you never know where that might lead, to what despairs, to what guilts. Perhaps to urges to smash everything around you, and that would mean trouble. And we don't want trouble. Anything but trouble. Nothing that might jeopardize our moral comfort. So then, eyes closed, ears stopped up, memory stopped up. Avoid making contact. Avoid becoming aware. Say you don't concern yourself with politics. Play bridge. Write a thesis on Crébillon fils.

Gokelaere also belonged to the world of tragedy. We didn't know it. Tragedy's a humble thing. It's taciturn. It doesn't fling its arms around as they do on stage. Tragedy is the pupil seated in the third row, beside the window. And a little later it will be that sickly figure in the crowd. That frail passerby in need of a haircut and wearing a cheap raincoat. Gokelaere lived tragically. There are men whom events chance to elevate to the level of tragedy, as a drowned body is pulled from the water. In his case, tragedy was his natural element, his personal climate. Clearsightedness, anguish, accusation, responsibility characterized his life. If I had truly looked I would have understood that. I would have sensed in him that vocation for anonymous calamity, I would have sensed the mass grave he was fated to. But I didn't look. I analyzed the authors in the program of studies, that's what I'm paid to do. I should add too that it is difficult, for the grown man to get through to the youngster. More so than to persons of any other age. There are those proud susceptibilities and those silences to be overcome, that mixture of grandiloquence and modesty, and that very vulgarity adolescence employs to protect itself from the encroachments of its elders. Even those who make the attempt soon give up. They take refuge in the mechanical carrying out of little tasks. Which doesn't stop them from singing in chorus, when the prizes are awarded for scholarship, about the noble mission of the Educator.

However, at fifteen, Gokelaere doesn't know about such things. He believes life is the way it's described in books. He dreams of a friendship grounded in seriousness and strength. Demands, oppositions are seeking shape inside him. He needs somebody who might be able to help him discern his certainties. This is what he hopes for from his teachers. That is their role, he says to himself. His mother is dead. Nothing to be expected from his classmates: he's disgusted by the good pupils, already nursing old men's ambitions, and the rest are deadening their minds in the interactions of a perfunctory eroticism. But there are the teachers, they ought to understand. There will surely be at least one of them who will understand. Or else what good are they? There will be at least one of them who will like him, to whom he will be able to say everything. Everything: he doesn't even know what he means by that—a wealth to be freed, a confusion to be untangled, an impulse to give form to . . . Children resign themselves unwillingly to doing without adults. And it was from me that he expected help. From me. It was later on that I found this out. For eventually one gets out of school, and then things are simpler. Having become a man, you are in a position to meet and make friends with other men. He had read something or other by me in some journal. He wrote to me. He told me about himself. I have kept all the letters in which he describes to me his great loneliness, and the timid and anxious hope he had placed in me. "Back in those days, I'd thought"—he wrote—"that you might become for me a sort of more advanced older classmate in whom one could have confided everything." But I failed to respond. I abandoned him to his loneliness, left him bitter with a bitterness that will be his for eternity. I am a teacher just like the others.

It's when it's all over that you understand. When it's too late, when there's nothing more to be done, when you can no longer do anything for anybody.

He's fifteen. He's twenty. He's alone. And solitude is not easily borne. For morons there are cafés. For believers, churches. But nowadays it's not often you run into believers. And they're not always pretty to look at. As empty for the most part as their churches, those gloomy churches where prayers produce only that murmur which lingers behind in empty seashells. So, for those not tempted by such things, card games or Mass, there are political parties. A party is first and foremost a touch of human warmth. The happiness of being men assembled together. Comrades. Camaraderie is something as strong as friendship. And it's more manly, more sober. Friendship extends just to one being. Camaraderie binds to a cause, to an undertaking, to an impassioned struggle in behalf of principle. It connects us to men not through what they are, but through what they do. Together you build a certain thing—a bridge or a road, or a world. They appeal to us, they do not appeal to us—we are not bothered by such questions. It's enough to know that a certain future has need both of them and of me, and that we have chosen to translate into reality an identical hope, an identical will, they and I, my comrades and I. There are twenty of us guys here in the back room of a bistro. Not what you'd call fancy surroundings. And the conversation isn't always what you'd call exciting. We talk about posters that have to be put up, leaflets to be distributed. And nevertheless there's more true fervor expended here than in all their churches. You feel confident here, assured. One man all by himself doesn't count for much, despite all his goodwill. A man who says "me"—the sound of his voice dies out right away. But when he says "the Party," his voice has the ring of solidity. "Me" is nothing against the world's hostility, the compactness of reality; less than a housefly pinging against a window pane. But the Party is something that has weight to it and which counts, and which breaks glass and the rest. You choose to align yourself with this force. Not so much because of the ideas you have. But to be with this force. You choose to join, and the ideas come afterward. You'd never be able to examine every single question and read everything. There will always be objections and replies, and replies to replies. You'd never get to the end of it. You need to take this violent, total plunge. You throw the whole of yourself bodily into it because that's where you have your place. The rebel inside the revolution. The conservative inside the establishment. Marx or Maurras don't have much to do with it. You've known from the very beginning in which camp you'd be fighting. Known it with a blind, organic knowledge; the way a plant knows sunlight.

Gokelaere grew up somewhere around Liévin or Hénin-Liétard, amid heavy industry's vehement landscapes which propose of the human condition a simple and terrible image. He belongs to all that is harsh and without hope, to the nights, to the crowds, to the violent working-class districts, to the dangerous brotherhoods of slavery and anger. He is on the side of rebellion. Not so much because of the books on political economy he forces himself to read; but through the workings of a loyalty rooted in the farthermost depths of his childhood and his breed. His companions can only be these untaught fellows who intend to change the world. He is with them: united, bound, committed. He will not back out. He has pledged himself. His promise will lead him as far as need be. All the way to that wall, in the morning, before which he will die at the hand of indifferent killers. All the way to that pit into which he will be thrown, among others who had pledged themselves too—or even who had made no pledges at all, who weren't even involved and won't have had a clue . . . The richness of those days to which he gave a meaning, a center. His comrades are there, it's all right. Everything's clear. We need you. If you can stop by the office. Some stuff to fix with the newspaper. You'll be able to straighten it out for us. Meeting's next Friday. . . .

But there are the evenings. The room you return to and where you find yourself. Not much fun finding yourself there. To come back to yourself as to a room that is always the same. The same helplessness, the same disgusts, the same dust and the same mold. During the day, it can be managed. You talk, you get bored, you do your work. But at night you sit facing your life and you are forced to look at it. Unless you go to the movies or the whorehouse. But Gokelaere is not the sort who runs away. I picture his evenings—the work table, the paper, the lamp. He's come home with newspapers in his pockets. He listens to the night. Nights, for a fellow like him, are something unwieldy and replete and populated. He feeds upon the sounds of those mining country nights. He deciphers their confused meanings. He collects the messages, everything that rises from the pits and the red brick mining villages. He is attuned to this enormous effort that causes the night to vibrate and cry, he is one with those thousands of night-time men, engulfed and toiling in the night, one with those men without names and faces into whose uncertain destiny he has chosen to disappear the way you disappear into darkness and death. He is plighted forevermore to those men in camps, in prisons, in torture chambers. His comrades. Plighted to that world of night and blood. Eleven o'clock, twelve o'clock—the moment when the world is most cruelly present to the attentive consciousness. At such times, commonplace objects admit of terrifying arrière-pensées. An alarm clock on a dresser makes its absurd noise that fills the room with hints and forebodings. A sound that reaches out to raise other sounds in the world of night and death:

Tick tock on the forehead, tick tock on the shoulder
Tick tock to the heart, tick tock in the guts,
Tick tock in the black sky, tick tock in the eyes,
Tick tock to the sweetness of your gaze,
Tick tock to the vignettes of days dead and gone,
Tick tock toward my mother's stiffened fingers,
Tick tock to the aches the length of spines . . .

Those are the kinds of things he writes, in the evening, in his room. Things he writes in order to deliver himself by means of words from the obsessive fears that come to him from the world. Which he writes awkwardly and obstinately, attempting, through poetry, to create himself. For he is not satisfied with himself. Nor with the action he is engaged in, and that's his secret torment. Eleven o'clock, midnight, the moment of great sincerity; the moment of weariness and relapse; of doubt. "For a long time I've had the impression that I must get out of something. Out of a swamp or a forest." Comrades don't protect you against that. Comrades are solid, yes they are, and dependable; but they provide no defense against that. One would like to live out the tragedy of all mankind, no other. But one has one's own tragedy, distinct from the tragedy shared by all, and to it one comes home every night. Your own inevitable, wretched tragedy. "That heaviness, that almost continual muck, that fragility." You've tried your best, but you've remained a poor man bogged down in weakness and disgust. Eleven o'clock, midnight, the time when you know you're alone, when you're a poor and lonely man.

> *Here the unbreathing plain,*
> *Years wavering far off;*
> *I've eaten bread in my ruin,*
> *I have mud all over my shoes,*
> *Grime under my nails.*

Those are the kinds of things he writes, things about weariness and solitude. There are the comrades. There are the hard facts and necessities of action. But even so, you're alone. Alone like the little boy whose dreams nobody knows. Alone like the corpse in the hole for corpses. Each evening the discouragements of solitude return.

> *The cagelike grocery*
> *Vomits its daily sugar.*
> *Find one's insect mantes anew.*

Each evening the consciousness of a guilt forms itself anew. "The distressing feeling of acting for action's sake, and in order to escape from myself." For the cause he serves will never be suspect in his view, just the personal motives that bring him to it. And finally you have no right to be alone. That's what he murmurs to himself, in the evenings. You have no right to conceal a part of yourself from your comrades. To pamper your own little ailments off in some private corner. Is partisan loyalty enough?

> *And our battle. Ours.*
> *Speak, speak, you, everyone.*
> *This hour will tell of it*
> *Only to those who haul no more.*
> *Comrades, forgive*
> *This hour that has pinned me down,*
> *This hour of old granite.*
> *Speak, speak, you, everyone.*
> *Against our land with no end*
> *And of harsh smoke of wood fires.*
> *Comrades, forgive me,*
> *I say nothing but for myself.*

There are some people who draw pride from their solitude. Gokelaere endures his like an incurable sin.

There's no defense against that; no remedy for that anguish of turning one's back upon communion in spite of yourself; of being caught between the giving of oneself and the quest for oneself, between fidelity and authenticity. He would express this in awkward, poignant poems. "The words chosen are more or less felicitous; you keep on looking." Poems he would send me, sometimes, hastily recopied, with mistakes in spelling. That's how he appeared to me. After his school days. He'd speak to me a little, in his letters, about his young wife, about a child born to them. That was in 1938, in 1939.

And now the story is over, it won't have gone on for long. Gokelaere was shot by a firing squad. Here's his name in an old newspaper. They came for him one morning, led him off in a clatter of heavy boots. On the brown paint of a corridor he will have read some obscene inscription, and that was the last sign he had from humankind. Now he has reached the ultimate point of human solitude. What that moment may have contained of despair or, who knows, of peace, no one will ever know. And there cannot be very many of us who care about such things. The comrades said: "Poor guy," or "The bastards." The time for words is past. A man walks between some huts and some barbed wire. He thinks about all that. The camp has its summer smell, its smell of urine and hot sand. The man looks, through the barbed wire, at the Russians being buried. Three hundred Russians per pit. How many does that amount to by now? He's a man who is no longer young. A man who is making up his accounts, since there is nothing else to do. He thinks about his life, about his profession. About the botched encounters, the friendships, about so many missed opportunities: it's always this you think about when you start reflecting on your life. All those precious possibilities, and you've let them slip through your fingers. Nothing to be proud of. And perhaps there wasn't any way to take hold of them. Can anyone know? Everything is such a tangle, there's no sorting the whole thing out. Or else it's all too simple. It all boils down to a question of arithmetic. As it does for the *Feldwebel* over there, with his pieces of paper and his cigar. The man pronounces: "Gokelaere." Without surprise, because you are no longer able to be surprised by anything. It's the effect of the times, you've seen too much. Gokelaere. A name they've printed in the newspapers, a name they must have posted in the subway corridors. A name scarcely more expressive than a number. Corpses are corpses, and there are too many of them for you to calculate what each one carried around during its lifetime in the way of dreams, of desires, and of sadness. I write his name, Gokelaere, the way you write a name on a cross. But nobody reads the names on crosses. And there isn't even a cross. There's nothing.

Translator's notes

Page 12. Georges Courteline, pseudonym of Georges Moineaux (1861-1929), popular comic writer whose works belonged to various genres and ranged in tone from broad farce to acerbic satire. Paul Déroulède (1846-1914), founder of the *Ligue des patriotes* in 1882. Exiled as a subversive, he also authored patriotic verse.

Page 12. Avenue de la Motte-Piquet in Paris runs before the main façade of the Ecole Militaire.

Page 16. Janson de Sailly, established in 1885, is a lycée that prepares for the *écoles spéciales*. The "special schools" are institutions of higher learning where an elite corps of students receive training for specialized careers.

Page 19. The Ecole Normale Supérieure, one of France's most prestigious "special schools," serves primarily to train lycée and university professors; many of its graduates have also distinguished themselves as writers and statesmen.

Page 41.   Louis Salavin is the protagonist of a cycle of five novels published between 1920 and 1932 by Georges Duhamel (1884-1966). These recount a clerk's failed quest to achieve spiritual salvation.

Page 61.   One of France's "écoles spéciales." The *Ecole Polytechnique* provides a program of scientific and technical training, whose graduates range from civil engineers to heads of state.

Page 81.   Charles Péguy (1873-1914), poet and essayist, whose patriotic amalgam of Christianity and socialism influenced a generation. His journal, *Les Cahiers de la Quinzaine* (1900-1915), was published out of his bookstore. He was a passionate Dreyfusard, and a fervent if non-practicing Roman Catholic. He died in the first Battle of the Marne in 1914.

Page 88.   Péguy attended but never took a degree from the *Ecole Normale*.

Page 94.   Ernest Lavisse (1842-1922), historian and authority on the seventeenth century, particularly known as general editor and part author of *Histoire de France depuis les origines jusqu'à la Révolution* (1900-1911) and *Histoire de France contemporaine depuis la Révolution jusqu'à la Paix de 1919* (1920-1922).

Page 94.   Gustave Lanson (1857-1934), literary historian and critic, director of the *Ecole Normale Supérieure*, and a professor at the Sorbonne. His *Histoire de la littérature française*, first published in 1894 and subsequently appearing in many further editions, enjoyed broad use and wide influence.

Page 95.   Charles Victor Langlois (1863-1929), historian of the Middle Ages.

Page 96.   Péguy's long poem *Eve*, published in 1914, was perhaps best known for its "Prière pour nous autres charnels" (Prayer for Us Creatures of Flesh and Blood), which contains a litany-like variation on the line "Heureux ceux qui sont morts pour la terre charnelle" (Fortunate are those who have died for the earth of flesh and blood).

Page 96. The Horatii were three legendary Roman brothers who swore to defend Rome by meeting three Alban adversaries, this despite the fact their sister was engaged to one of them. The classic story of triumphant patriotic duty was immortalized in French tradition both by Corneille's play *Horace* and by Jacques-Louis David's painting *Oath of the Horatii*. It served as an example of Republican virtue in the French Revoilutionm. Likewise, the "soldiers of Year II" refers to the massive "people's army" that was raised during the Terror to combat France's external enemies; Year II ran from September 1793 to September 1794.

Page 104. Claude-Prosper Jolyot de Crébillon (1707-1777), author of tales and dialogues with libertine themes.

Page 104. Lycée studies conclude with a national examination: candidates who pass it receive their *baccalauréat*, which qualifies them to enter the university.